MERGERS, ACQUISITIONS, AND EMPLOYEE ANXIETY

MERGERS, ACQUISITIONS, AND EMPLOYEE ANXIETY

A Study of Separation Anxiety in a Corporate Context

Joseph H. Astrachan

New York
Westport, Connecticut
London

Library of Congress Cataloging-in-Publication Data

Astrachan, Joseph H. (Joseph Henry)
  Mergers, acquisitions, and employee anxiety : a study of
separation anxiety in a corporate context / Joseph H. Astrachan.
    p.   cm.
  Includes bibliographical references.
  ISBN 0-275-93568-X (alk. paper)
  1. Consolidation and merger of corporations—Psychological
aspects.   2. Separation (Psychology)   I. Title.
HD2746.5.A88   1990
158.7—dc20   90-30002

Library of Congress Catalog Card Number: 90-30002
ISBN: 0-275-93568-X

First published in 1990

Praeger Publishers, One Madison Avenue, New York, NY 10010
An imprint of Greenwood Publishing Group, Inc.

Printed in the United States of America

∞

The paper used in this book complies with the
Permanent Paper Standard issued by the National
Information Standards Organization (Z39.48-1984).

10 9 8 7 6 5 4 3 2 1

TP

For Libby

Contents

Illustrations

EXHIBITS

FIGURES

TABLES

Preface

Separation, especially in the context of mergers and acquisitions, is a stressful experience. People frequently do not wish to consider the painful aspects of separation, preferring to focus on its benefits and rational causes. "Always look on the bright side" is a common strategy for coping with personal stress caused by others' tragedies. To adequately consider this topic, one must keep personal stress needs in check and have a balanced outlook. It is therefore useful for readers to take a few minutes to reflect on personal and career-related separations, including both the most traumatic and the most pleasant, before reading this book.

The following narrative passages are helpful in promoting introspection. The first is from Ed Joyce's (1988) book *Prime Times, Bad Times*. The second was written by one of my more insightful students.

Ed Joyce employed rich detail in describing his experiences during a time when CBS was under continual take-over threats. During that time CBS used many tactics to fend off unwanted take-overs. Among those was a constant attempt to increase profitability, including the use of early retirement plans and layoffs. Joyce, former president of CBS News, started this passage with a recollection of the day he announced layoffs at CBS News:

The next day was every bit as terrible as I'd feared. A day of incalculable sadness at CBS News. A number of people had accepted the early-retirement offer and some recent job openings had not been filled, so the total number of those laid off had been reduced to seventy-four. But this was no consolation to those who were now out of work. Everyone had old friends who would be going, and the coming departure of the early retirees was equally regretted. . . .

As I walked through the halls that day I could sense the hurt and the hostility around me. At one point I walked past Marian Glick. . . . She was among those retiring early. She must have sensed something in my face, because she walked over to me and kissed me. The memo I'd sent to the organization describing the scope and reasons behind the layoffs had just been distributed.

"I know how terrible you feel," Marian said.

I walked into my office, closed the door, and sat alone for several minutes before I could continue. (pp. 504-5)

Of his entire experience during this period, Joyce wrote, "Increasingly, I felt like someone trying to do the sidestroke in a whirlpool" (p. 510). Joyce's experiences at CBS led him to reflect upon his childhood separations:

By 1940 the Depression was ending and California seemed the best place to find work. My folks gathered together for sale whatever we owned, including the Navajo rugs and jewelry they'd loved and wanted to keep for themselves. We were off on a journey which would repeat itself over and over again for the next ten years. . . . I came to like the backseat of old cars and staring out the window at passing farmland, with rows of planted crops like daddy longlegs running alongside you. Always on our way to someplace else. (p. 132)

The second passage, from a perceptive student, explores how current feelings and behavior have roots in early life experiences. The excerpt begins with her realization of the importance that separation anxiety was playing in her life:

I hesitated at first to offer up the uncharacteristic and recent bickering that I was experiencing with my long-time boyfriend as an example to the class of irrational behavior caused by separation anxiety. I was reluctant to both have my personal life dissected and more importantly, I think, to admit to myself that I was not adequately dealing with separation anxiety currently. I knew deep down, however, that my behavior towards my boyfriend was resulting at least in part from separation anxiety and I finally forced myself to share my experiences with the class.

I did not anticipate the reverberations that the verbalization of my thoughts would set off inside my head and those of others. As I talked and listened to the responses of other students, I believe I began the process of more clearly recognizing the effects of separation anxiety on my past and present behavior. My description of how I had begun to behave with my boyfriend since I had accepted the idea that our separation next year was inevitable prompted other members of the class to talk about similar experiences. . . . We talked about our shared perceptions that the anger we often generated against individuals as a result of separation anxiety and in preparation for impending separation was easier to handle than the sadness we all felt would accompany a "civil" separation. At one point, one of the class members stated that, "I intuitively feel that anger is easier to deal with than sadness of longing, and that is why I sometimes behave irrationally when I must separate from someone I love." I found myself agreeing with that statement. . . . Up until that point I had taken for granted my method of dealing with separation and did not yet realize that my behavior toward my boyfriend was part of a familiar pattern of dealing with separation anxiety that I had established in childhood. It had never occurred to me that people could end romantic relationships on a pleasant note. In my mind relationships of that nature only ended when turmoil existed to justify ending them. At that moment I was not aware of the fact that I had recently begun a process of creating a heightened level of tension in my relationships with many of my college friends, my parents, and especially my boyfriend in order to fulfill that requirement for severing relationships that existed in my mind.

I realize now that separation anxiety was also carrying over into other aspects of my life—I had noticed a dramatic increase in my normal level of procrastination as well as the development of a very uncharacteristic pattern of non-decision making in my daily life. I had noticed these troubling developments but had stopped short of recognizing these behavioral patterns as reactions to the separations I would soon face as a graduating senior. I attributed my growing indecisiveness to other sources such as a wide array of options, lack of adequate information, and time constraints.

When I began to reflect upon the separations that I had experienced in my life and how they might affect my current perceptions, attitudes, and mechanisms for coping with separation, it became clear that my family life as a young child had a profound impact not only on my ability to separate but my willingness to attach as well. Coping with separation from familiar people and places was a process that began early in life for me. My father worked for a government agency in my youth and, as a result, I had attended five different schools in different states and countries by the time I entered fifth grade. . . . I began to develop mechanisms of attaching and separating that I believed would minimize the pain I had felt upon my first separation from familiar people and surroundings.

When I think of the transition periods before and after each of our family's relocations, I recall anger, confusion, and an increasing dependence on members of my family for emotional support. In order to cope with the pain I associated with separation, I developed a pattern of becoming angry or upset with my childhood companions prior to my family's departure, of withdrawing from them and finally turning to my brother, sisters, and parents for social fulfillment and emotional support.

These excerpts were offered to help prepare readers for the difficult issues of mergers, acquisitions, and separation anxiety that follow. Understanding one's personal experiences and reactions to this topic is paramount to gaining insight into the feelings, motivations, and behaviors of others.

Acknowledgments

In his poem *The Love Song of J. Alfred Prufrock*, T. S. Eliot (1934) wrote, "I have measured out my life with coffee spoons" (p. 5). Since beginning this research I, on the other hand, have been measuring out and sweetening my life with the large and small separations I have confronted.

While I always learn and am moved by separations I have seen or studied, personal separations have always had the greatest impact on me. During the past ten years I have repeatedly witnessed and experienced separation anxiety firsthand. While at Yale I contended with graduate students who moved on before finishing their studies and graduate students who left after receiving their terminal degrees; with staff who retired and staff who were promoted or transferred; with faculty members who left of their own will, faculty members who departed because they were denied tenure or promotion, and those who were asked to leave. In my last years there, dramatic changes at the School of Organization and Management resulted in the announced departures of all nontenured organizational behavior faculty members. That decree was retracted and replaced by one of less certainty concerning their futures. Faculty and staff members of the school still refer to those events as the "hostile take-over at Yale."

On an even more personal level, I have had to deal with extended family members who have passed on unexpectedly and family who have moved locations while beginning new phases in their lives. I have developed an extensive inventory of separation experiences, all of which have been unique in some way or another and all of which have caused me to feel and behave somewhat differently. The effects of these many separations and the yearning to understand them are largely responsible for my desire to study and write about topics that deal with separation anxiety.

The stimulus for this book also came from my growing awareness of how separation anxiety affected others. The purpose of this volume is to complete the loop and share my learning with others. My particular concern for people facing mergers or acquisitions comes from my belief that they are in one of the most widespread anxiety-producing situations in corporate America. How separation anxiety affects emotions and behavior during mergers and acquisitions is the focus of this book.

If this book helps people to begin examining their own experiences, it will have been a success. Hopefully, this book will stimulate others to think more broadly about the topic of separation. The ultimate aim is that readers will find it helpful in managing personal separations and those experienced by others.

I am grateful to those who have helped me with this research, and I thank the students who participated in this study. Teaching students and learning from them is an experience I cherish. Four teachers I thank are Jim Herbert, Ivan Lansberg, Clay Alderfer, and David Berg. They formed a core advisory and support group for this research and for my own professional development. In particular, it was Jim Herbert's suggestion that I consider introducing a separation exercise to the class we were teaching at Yale. It was during a discussion with Clay Alderfer that I began to think of how important these issues are to behavior during mergers and acquisitions. I thank Ellen Kossek for introducing me to her students at Michigan State University and for her advice.

I thank Marta O'Rourke-Crawford and Dorlie Smith for their tireless assistance in preparing this manuscript.

I also thank my family, my brothers David and Michael, my sister Ellen, and especially my parents, Boris and Batja. I believe that our shared experiences and closeness as a family gave me a keen sensitivity to separation anxiety. My parents' own childhood experiences of change, loss and, feelings of separateness exerted a powerful influence on me and my feelings about separation. My mother emigrated with her parents and brother from Holland at a young age, leaving her childhood friends and much family behind. My father was orphaned before he graduated college and was without roots until he met my mother. In addition, I especially thank Boris for introducing me to the field of organizational behavior through his writing and for always being available to kibitz me at every step over a friendly game of pinochle.

Last and most, I thank Libby, my partner-in-life. She has supported and encouraged me in every way possible. She has been a secure base in my life, helping me with my many separations and attachments. We have vowed to have and to hold one another eternally.

Introduction

In recent years we have seen a remarkable growth in the number of mergers and acquisitions in the world. It seems like every type of organization in every industry is vulnerable. Companies employing hundreds of thousands of people are now bought and sold practically on a daily basis. Negotiations for sales and purchases occur more frequently. It is even more common for sale and purchase rumors to be widespread. Euphemistically it is said that companies being considered for sale or purchase have been "put into play." The number of people who have been directly affected by a merger or acquisition is substantial. Yet, with all the human consequences, the psychological, emotional, and behavioral impact of mergers and acquisitions have remained largely unexplored.

This research represents one of the first systematic investigations into the psychological effects of mergers and acquisitions. It is especially novel in three ways. First, it uses the concept of separation anxiety to help understand emotional and behavioral reactions to mergers and acquisitions. Second, it explores how relationships and behavior within groups shape reactions to mergers and acquisitions. And third, it systematically develops and tests theory using a rigorously controlled mergers and acquisitions simulation. Throughout the book, case reports and individual experiences are reported— in people's own words when possible—to illuminate and enrich our understanding of mergers, acquisitions, and separation anxiety.

The progression of the book is from the general to the specific and then back to the general. Mergers, acquisitions, and anxiety are presented initially to familiarize the reader with the topic. The first section is designed to help the reader begin thinking about the connections between mergers and acquisitions and anxiety. The aim is to prepare the reader for the more detailed exploration of the specific anxiety—separation anxiety—that follows.

Separation anxiety is a distinctive anxiety associated with the frightening situation of having a relationship change drastically or end. It is the cognitive emotional state that is caused by cues of impending separation. It occurs before separation actually takes place. Separation anxiety can occur when separation is only implied. For example, unexplained changes in behavior and rumors can cause intense separation anxiety. It is characterized by strong emotions and atypical behavior that usually occur prior to a separation.

Following the initial presentations, specific hypotheses are generated by augmenting the theory of separation anxiety with group and boundary dynamics concepts. In order to do this, the focus of the research narrows considerably from the wide angle of the theory. The well-defined situation of small work groups in a stable organization are chosen for study. The hypotheses concern whether separation anxiety is stimulated by the anticipated exit of a group member(s) or other groups in an organization; how responses to separation anxiety are affected by the number of group members leaving; and how individual experiences are influenced by whether the individual is leaving or staying in the group.

With hypotheses made, the mergers and acquisitions simulation is introduced and connected to the underlying theory and hypotheses. The simulation was designed from an amalgamation of real life experiences. In the simulation, participants were placed in small, five- or six-member groups. They were told that they comprised a senior human resources policy group in a stable organization. After learning of the impending merger and who in the group was to leave, they performed the same decision-making task. The number of people staying in and leaving the group was different depending on the experimental condition to which the group was assigned. Questionnaire data were collected concerning individual attitudes towards the group, group process, and affective state. Questionnaire data were analyzed using a repeated measures experimental design. Written narratives of experiences during the simulation were also obtained. One hundred and nineteen people participated in three separate simulations. Two were held on the East Coast and one in the Midwest. The ages of participants ranged from 19 to 56, averaging about 23.

The quantitative and qualitative results of the research are then presented and discussed. It was found that small manipulations have profound effects on individuals and groups. The results indicated that the effects of separation anxiety are influenced by the number of people separating. Separation anxiety often produced stress because individuals increased the strength of their attachments without preparing for separation. This made separation more emotionally stressful. Group process, individual emotions, and individual attitudes toward the group were all affected by impending separation. Further, prior separation experiences greatly influenced later responses to separation anxiety. Most notably, prior separations that had a traumatic quality were related to more disturbing emotional responses to subsequent separations. The results also suggested that separation anxiety can be managed, reducing negative effects while emphasizing positive aspects.

After the results discussion the book returns to the theory to modify and expand it as the results indicate. Issues such as the basic mechanism of separation anxiety, the impact of the setting, previous experiences, and the characteristics of the separation itself are revisited. Finally, the implications of separation anxiety for managers dealing with its effects are examined in mergers, acquisitions, intergroup dynamics in general including race and gender dynamics, and other common managerial circumstances.

The issues presented here are timely and clearly warrant further investigation. The purpose of this book is to open ever wider the discussion of the psychological effects of mergers and acquisitions, including separation anxiety, and their consequences for organizations.

MERGERS, ACQUISITIONS, AND EMPLOYEE ANXIETY

1

Mergers, Acquisitions, and Separation Anxiety

This research began with three questions: Why does behavior change during mergers and acquisitions? Are these changes predictable? Can we reduce behaviors that lead to negative consequences, while accentuating beneficial behaviors? These questions grew from examples such as the following.

While observing a group whose company had just acquired a sizeable competitor, I was perplexed by the degree to which people were actively denying the potential hazards of their situation. They claimed to believe that their jobs were not in serious jeopardy. However, they appeared to display great uneasiness and tension. As the video display monitors flickered around us I noticed a relevant news item. I asked if they knew that their firm planned to layoff at least 6,000 employees as a result of the acquisition. I was then told the rumor that 10,000 would be let go. Another individual began to talk about how many of "their" (the competitor's) people would be hurt personally. They then stopped the discussion as abruptly as I had started it. It was clear that the merger was having a profound emotional effect on people in the office. How the situation was influencing their work was less evident.

The above took place several years ago. Subsequently, that company has had numerous layoffs. People were upset each time. However, all did not respond in the same way to layoff news. Some became angry and somewhat destructive, others became withdrawn and increasingly nonproductive, and others seemed to be inviting "burn-out" as they threw themselves into their work with ever greater zeal.

This example provides a brief illustration of the kinds of behavior changes we might see arising during mergers and acquisitions. In order to understand why these changes occur we need to move beyond the misleading economic notion that people behave according to a complex function of expected future earning power. Indeed, we are compelled to explore the psychological underpinnings of behavior. Over a century of psychological study has taught us that we cannot understand emotions and behavior during frightening situations, such as mergers and acquisitions, without the concept of anxiety. Understanding employee anxiety is critical to any explanation of behavior change during mergers and acquisitions.

There is vast evidence that employee anxiety skyrockets during mergers and acquisitions. One major source of anxiety is the fear that relationships will be severed, as a result of layoffs, transfers, or the restructuring of work. Of the many anxieties that have been researched, the most applicable is separation anxiety. Separation anxiety is a specific anxiety pivotal to our understanding of how people are affected by mergers and acquisitions.

Separation anxiety can be defined in a brief and technical manner as the cognitive-emotional state that accompanies impending separation. That is to say that it takes place before actual separation. Separation anxiety encompasses the behavioral and emotional reactions to impending physical or psychological distancing.

Whenever separation from another is likely, separation anxiety is also likely. Strong emotions and unusual behavior are usually evidenced prior to a separation. For example, old friends may fight savagely. Separation anxiety takes place whenever a relationship with someone or something important is altered. It occurs with each life transition. Examples include a child leaving home, the death of a pet, relocation, a loved one leaving, or the end of a relationship. In organizations, separation anxiety occurs routinely before retirements, promotions, transfers, individual sick leaves, leaves of absence, layoffs, firings, organized strikes, divestitures, corporate restructurings and consolidations, and mergers and acquisitions (the focus of this work). Though it occurs frequently and with great force, its sources and effects have not been thoroughly investigated. Why do we not know more about separation anxiety? Perhaps it is too powerful and too uncomfortable.

The effects of separation anxiety are complex. For example, suppose that a work group learns that one of its members has been asked to leave, as often occurs during mergers and acquisitions. What emotions will be aroused? Will the impending separation cause people to behave differently? Will it interfere with their ability to work individually and together? Will the announcement of a separation affect their relationships? How will they deal with the fact that one of their own has been asked to leave? What happens to the person who is asked to leave? Will anyone come to his or her aid and offer support? And what will happen to those who remain? All will be affected by the impact of separation.

There are good reasons to assume that separation anxiety is stimulated by organizational mergers and acquisitions. While mergers represent, at some level, a coming together of organizations and people, during mergers people are usually laid-off, fired, transferred, demoted, promoted, given new reporting relationships (new bosses and subordinates), reorganized, restructured, and cutback often without warning and without sufficient time to prepare or make alternative arrangements. Many authors (e.g., Callahan, 1986; Mirvis & Marks, 1986; Hayes, 1979; DeMeuse, 1986) have reported that mergers and acquisitions heighten expectations of separation and result in actual separations. One senior executive who was in the midst of a merger reported to me, "I'm experienced at this job, yet I feel like I don't quite know what I'm doing. I wonder how the newer [people at my level] are handling this merger." During a merger or acquisition, even those not personally affected by any of these activities will know of people who are.

Before launching into an investigation of separation anxiety and how it can aid our understanding of behavior during mergers and acquisitions, it is helpful to cull prior literature for added wisdom. Most writing about mergers and acquisitions concerns post-merger behavior, including case reports, the effects of clashing cultures, and how-to proscriptions designed to help managers cope with mergers that have already taken place. There have been several notable exceptions to this trend.

Presaging the application of separation anxiety to mergers and acquisitions are Mitchell Marks and Philip Mirvis. Marks (1982) noted that the two most important factors associated with increased stress during mergers are uncertainty and insecurity. He found that news of a merger stimulates "personal or vicarious recollections of merger horror stories" (p. 41). He indicated that even when upper management promises no changes employees are suspicious and fearful. Such responses are characteristic of an anxious state. Marks also related that psychological denial is a prevalent coping mechanism for managers. Denial occurred in such forms as, "beliefs and rumors that the board of directors would never approve a takeover," and, "the refusal to accept and come to terms with the new situation" (p. 41). Anxiety researchers have also identified denial as a primary means for coping with anxiety.

Working as a team, Marks and Mirvis (1985) identified common behaviors which they labeled the "merger syndrome": "Basically, the merger syndrome is triggered by the often unavoidable unsettled conditions in the earliest days and months following the combination and encompasses the executives' stressful reactions and development of crisis-management orientation" (p. 50). They indicated that part of this syndrome involves a fight/flight reaction (Bion, 1961) to stress. Employees of merging organizations were said to become either overly hostile and aggressive, or withdrawn and despondent. They also found that individuals in teams tended to cope with stress by banding together in a manner that can foster poor decision making and "groupthink" (Janis, 1972). All of these reactions are characteristic ways in which individuals and groups cope with anxiety (Jaques, 1974).

Mirvis and Marks (1986) also discovered that social support helped people cope with stress created by mergers. They indicated that supported people displayed less stress and had fewer suspicions and fears about the behavior of upper management. However, Buono et al. (1985) reported widespread resentment and distrust of upper management in mergers where trust was broken. These observations are highly supportive of the proposition that mergers and acquisitions foster employee anxiety.

ILLUSTRATIONS OF MERGERS AND ACQUISITIONS

The following excerpts from published articles and various conversations with managers before and after mergers are provided to illustrate the feelings, thoughts, and behaviors that emerge as a result of merger activity. These examples help shape our understanding of how people cope with separation anxiety during mergers and acquisitions and help us to identify specific coping behaviors.

Harshbarger (1987) provided the following recollection of his experiences during a merger that led to his departure from Sealy, Incorporated. He described the overall depressive reactions which employees experienced:

On the Tuesday before Thanksgiving, we were shocked to learn that Sealy, Inc., had just been sold to the Ohio Mattress company. . . . Happy Thanksgiving. By the end of December, the company had undergone a takeover. Merry Christmas. My senior colleagues and I greeted the New Year with foreboding, and with good reason: by mid-March, most of us were unemployed. (p. 340)

He used dramatic metaphors to describe the dynamics set in motion by mergers and acquisitions:

The announcement of a takeover brings life in a corporate office to a halt. There is shock, disbelief, tears, and long faces and slumped shoulders. A psychological time bomb has been dropped. As in the aftermath of the explosion of a neutron bomb, physical property remains intact, but most life, or in this case work, ceases.

Once the paralysis wears off, usually in a matter of a few days, a semblance of normality returns. People come to work, write memos, continue projects, and hold meetings. But nothing happens. Important decisions take longer and longer to make and, eventually, aren't made at all. Who knows what the new owners will want?

For the sake of analogy, imagine that it is France, 1940. Paris has just fallen. The occupying forces are coming and the radio daily reports their troop movements. The end of a way of life is near. We can only wait.

And imagine seeing some of our colleagues trying to anticipate the whims of the occupying force and scheming to ingratiate themselves with them. It is Vichy France psychologically revisited. (p. 341)

War metaphors that express intense anxiety are commonly used by those who have experienced the threat of a merger.

The following quotes were offered by one senior executive shortly after a rumor that her company was about to be taken over spread throughout the financial community. First, she described the way in which humor was being used to simultaneously recognize and avoid the perilous situation: "Humor is rampant. People are coping via humor. Some are joking that they'll turn our building into a K-Mart Boutique. It's totally out of control." Later, she talked about the banding together effect of the merger rumor: "People who don't usually talk to each other are talking. Although they talk about it only in the realm of the bizarre, in an off-handed tone." While reflecting on the level of despair in the organization she also offered some interesting beliefs of the feelings held by top management:

I guess you just have to throw up your hands and hope for the best. The people [those high up in the corporate hierarchy] who do know [exactly what's going on] are probably tearing their hair out. I saw [the chairman and CEO] walking the halls for the first time in months and he looked like he had a lot on his mind [laughter].

It's like when your whole world might be turned upside-down, everybody's [long pause]. You know when you think about nuclear weapons, you can't really think about it because the consequences are so dramatic, but when it's imminent, you have to cope and get work done and people work together! You have to have a lot of faith in your board of directors.

Employees in this workplace were somewhat overcome. They displayed a wide range of emotion. While the merger news apparently unleashed an abundance of nervous energy in this organization, others have experienced a saddening effect.

In her consulting work, Sinetar (1981) had many occasions to view the effects of merger announcements. In the excerpt below she reported the paralyzing, depressing, and intensely emotional consequences of merger news:

Initially, workers experienced shock, disbelief and grief, as if someone had died in their family. These emotions were followed by resentment, anger and/or depression. Only in the final phases of the merger period (many months later) did the majority come to a workable, healthy resolution within themselves.

One Thursday morning a company in which I had been consulting for about a year unexpectedly announced its plans for a merger over the company intercom. People could be seen standing in the halls in small groups as if in shock. The only other time I'd personally observed people in similar states of disbelief was shortly after the announcement that President John F. Kennedy had been shot. Then, as in this case, people stood about numbly, some with tears of disbelief in their eyes. Days, weeks, months later they referred back to that original moment in ways that said, "I still remember what I was doing during that tragic announcement—I can still feel myself turning numb in the midst of my activity." Employees referred back to the merger announcement as "Black Thursday." (p. 864)

The following case does not deal specifically with a merger though it does concern one of the more frequent results of a merger: plant closings. This case is particularly appropriate because it describes multiple and somewhat overlapping ranges of behaviors. In Berenbeim's (1985) study of the closing of GTE's Lenkurt facility he summarized the prevalent psychological and behavioral reactions, including humor, overeating, and denial:

The drawn-out nature of the multiple closings elicited a good deal of gallows humor. One department built a grave-yard, with tombstones bearing the name of each employee.. . . .

Another form of release was overeating, which resulted in the only pervasive health complaint—weight gain. As the work force got smaller, the cafeteria supplier complained that twice the usual number of doughnuts, pies and cakes were needed to slake the survivors' radically changed eating habits. Cigarette sales also went up.

A few avoided the reality and pretended it was a bad dream. One man went to the head of the closing team and said: "I know I'm not getting laid-off, but every once in a while I'll wake up in the middle of the night and my stomach is turning. I have this horrible feeling that I am going to lose my job." (pp. 43-44)

One outcome of these behaviors is that they enabled employees to momentarily escape their frightening reality. In some instances this was only partially achieved by pretending that it was others who should be afraid.

The following piece is important because it discusses the long term consequences of merger rumors. Writing about the after shocks of successfully averting a take-over at Phillips Petroleum Company, Solomon (1989) noted that even the slightest cues of another take-over caused rampant anxiety. He stated that even the company's rebounding profitability, "hasn't stopped the rumors, or the anxiety, in Bartlesville" (p. 1).

For a company and a town that have been the target of two wrenching takeover battles, fear can give life to even the shakiest notions. That's what is happening in Bartlesville these days. The place is running scared, and enemies—often more imagined than real—appear to lurk in every shadow. "This is the biggest rumor mill I've ever seen in my life," sighs Gene Prunty, whose barbershop is across the street from the Phillips building. "People are still afraid."

To a unique degree, Phillips dramatizes the fear and loathing spawned by takeovers—both before they materialize and long after they have been defeated. Shaken employees see their jobs being traded on Wall Street. Once bruised by a raid, they become obsessed with the possibility of new threats, to the point where a kind of corporate post-traumatic-stress syndrome sets in. (p. 1)

Of the many effects of the heightened state of anxiety, Phillips' chairman indicated that it, "is affecting our ability to retain and motivate employees"

(p. 1). This piece suggests that long-term effects of merger rumors are more complex for multiple events than for single incidents. Specifically, it indicates that repeated bouts with merger and take-over attempts intensify emotional and behavioral reactions to subsequent merger rumors.

The evolving theory of separation anxiety can add a great deal to the intuitive understanding provided by the above examples. Ultimately, this will lead to a greater ability to manage employees during mergers, acquisitions, and organizational change in general. We now turn to a theoretical exploration of anxiety and separation anxiety. Following that, the expected effects of separation anxiety on work groups during mergers and acquisitions will be explored.

2

Anxiety, Separation Anxiety, and Behavior in Groups

Fundamental to understanding behavior during mergers and acquisitions is the concept of anxiety. In order to predict how separation anxiety functions at the individual and group levels, we must first explore anxiety in general and separation anxiety in particular. In this chapter the general concept of anxiety is discussed in order to illuminate the causes and effects of separation anxiety. Knowledge of how anxiety and separation anxiety function at the individual level serves as a foundation on which a theory of separation anxiety at the group level can be constructed. Group dynamics concepts are then introduced to provide an additional ingredient necessary for understanding how separation anxiety and group dynamics shape one another. The chapter concludes with the development of specific hypotheses about how separation anxiety functions at the individual and group levels.

ANXIETY IN GENERAL

Anxiety is not a new concept. It has, however, been frequently called one of the most difficult to define (Lewis, 1970). Anxiety can be defined as a psychological, social, and biological phenomenon resulting from a consciously or unconsciously perceived threat to the individual (cf. Lesse, 1970; May, 1977). Providing a more visceral definition, William James (1902) described the feeling of anxiety as, "the pit of insecurity beneath the surface of life."

Sigmund Freud (1925) identified two forms of anxiety: automatic and signal anxiety. Automatic anxiety is produced by a state of over excitation, such as a traumatic experience. Signal anxiety occurs when there is consciously or unconsciously perceived to be an impending threatening situation. Also capable of triggering signal anxiety are nonspecific cues rooted in unconscious memories associated with past traumatic events. For example, an odor that was present during a past frightening event can cause and amplify an anxious state when smelled years later. This is akin to Skinner's (1941) findings concerning conditioned stimuli.

Once established, even slight cues of previous traumatic events can bring about an anxious response (Hofer, 1975; May, 1977). Lesse (1982) has shown that increasing stress using sources unrelated to an existing anxious state, such as via drugs, significantly increases symptoms of anxiety. The debilitating effects of anxiety may be greatly increased by other sources of stress. This is particularly important for mergers and acquisitions where the daily responsibilities of employees are already producing high levels of stress.

Anxiety is generally displayed through actions that are inconsistent with previous behavior. For example, a normally gregarious person might become withdrawn or a self-assured person might become insecure. Anxiety often causes us to behave in an apparently irrational manner because we are responding to feelings born out of past experiences and biological and genetic predispositions. This means that anxiety leads to reduced attention to the immediate situation and increased reactivity to internal emotional states. It is easy to envision how anxiety can wreak havoc with a group and organization if it is not detected and managed.

SEPARATION ANXIETY

In building a theory of separation anxiety it is helpful to consider evidence of its existence. Existing evidence comes from work in three areas of study at the individual level: animals, children, and adults. Most of that research did not directly explore separation anxiety. However, by allowing us to see its effects, the following evidence is nonetheless helpful in understanding how separation anxiety operates.

Animals

The largest body of animal research directly relevant to separation anxiety has focused on the study of young nonhuman primates. One of the major innovators and initiators of this work was H. F. Harlow (1958, 1974). In a series of experiments, Harlow alone and with his colleagues (1959, 1965) demonstrated the immediate and long term effects of separation on young and infant monkeys. These include a range of potentially life threatening behaviors such as depression, symptoms similar to autism, long term social difficulties, avoidance of social contact, excessive fearfulness, internally and externally directed aggression, lack of appropriate sexual behaviors in adulthood, and other severe behavioral deficits.

Others have investigated specific factors that affect reactions to separation. Lewis et al. (1976) noted that reactions become more intense as the number of separations increases. This is in direct opposition to the commonly held belief that animals, including man, become "desensitized" to painful situations. Young et al. (1973) found that the effects of infant separation could be somewhat alleviated by younger normally reared monkeys which they termed "monkey psychiatrists." The monkey psychiatrists provided emotional and social support through a host of intimate behaviors such as clinging and grooming. Young and his colleagues also showed that monkeys who had traumatic separation experiences as infants had different reactions to adolescent and adult separation than did their normally raised peers. Notably, monkeys who had early separation experiences responded to later separation with depression and withdrawal, while those who had no early separation experience responded with protest and animation.

Other animal evidence suggests that separation anxiety is innate and biologically determined and therefore something that can never be eliminated. Examining brain evolution from a biological perspective, MacLean (1985) noted, "The separation call perhaps ranks as the earliest and most basic mammalian vocalization" (p. 405). He further explained, "It is an innate sound that originates as a result of one of the most distressful mammalian conditions, namely separation" (p. 415). He discovered the existence of a part of the brain which is devoted to separation calls. MacLean suggested that only mammals have a separation call. Earlier, Lawick-Goodall (1968) observed that young free-ranging chimpanzees, up to seven years of age, can quickly summon their mothers with a separation scream. She also observed marked anxiety in young chimpanzees when briefly separated from their mothers. Bowlby (1973a) has speculated that separation anxiety has a profound survival value and is the result of evolutionary processes.

Children

A universal experience for parents is a child who cries and becomes upset every time a parent is about to leave the room. Reactions such as this stimulated the first modern studies of separation anxiety. In many ways, the study of separation anxiety began with the studies of children and the development of the mother-child relationship. Evidence about the existence of separation anxiety in preschool children led to the development of important psychoanalytic theory (Freud, 1909). Rank (1924) insisted that the prototype for all anxiety comes from the trauma of birth, which is the first separation of child from mother. Klein (1948) identified two sources for separation anxiety;

both of which concern the child's belief that he or she can control the separation of his or her mother. Depressive anxiety results from the child's belief that he or she has destroyed his or her mother, and persecutory anxiety results from the child's belief that separation is punishment for some wrongdoing. The behavior of the child during the departure and return of a parent wàs seen as largely determined by which of these two anxieties the child harbored.

Important early clinical studies of separation anxiety in children were sponsored by Anna Freud (1937, 1945). Burlingham and Freud (1942, 1944) witnessed extreme reactions of children in the process of being separated from their mothers at nursery school. In a series of experimental and clinical studies, Mahler et al. (1975) investigated the process of the child's development of an awareness of being separate from mother. These investigators observed several connections between how the child develops during this process and subsequent behavior. They stated that a fundamental source of psychological turmoil is the child's desire to simultaneously move away from and maintain contact with mother. They found that children who underwent premature separations from their mothers, that is separation occurring before psychological readiness, had increased difficulty in separating from their mothers throughout this process. They also noticed that a rejecting mother increased the difficulty of separation. Mothers who vigorously pushed their attention-seeking children away seemed to develop children who became extremely agitated when their mother was leaving.

Mahler and her colleagues identified several early mechanisms for coping with the discomfort and distress of separation. Hyperactivity and restlessness were seen as a defense against sadness due to separation. Overidentification with another person was seen as a way of coping with the increased separation due to the birth of a sibling. Frustration, tantrums, and helplessness were all seen as reactions to the problem of the child's wanting to simultaneously separate from and remain attached to mother.

Systematic experimentation by Rheingold and Eckerman (1970) uncovered a linear relationship between age, anxiety, and the distance that a child will travel from his or her mother. Studying children from infancy through the toddler period, they found that anxiety decreased and distance traveled increased as a linear function of the child's age. They were unclear as to whether the decrease in anxiety was due to biological changes in the child or changes in the relationship between mother and child. One could expect that as the level of security and trust between mother and child increased so did the child's comfort with separating from mother to go exploring (cf. Bowlby, 1988b). Their research suggests that comfort with separating is tantamount to exploration and thus creative innovation.

Yarrow (1967) found that by the age of eight months every infant he studied suffered from mild to severe separation anxiety. This strongly suggests a biological root to separation anxiety. Doris et al. (1980) studied preschool children and found separation anxiety to varying degrees in all the children they studied. They distinguished between children who had severely and mildly anxious reactions to separation. They found that the intensely anxious children were more aggressive than the less anxious children during interactions with peers. Children with high levels of separation anxiety also performed less well on a battery of cognitive tasks, both when their parents were present and when they were not. In sum, the work concerning children indicates that separation anxiety is prevalent, and has profound emotional and behavioral effects, and that separation experiences affect subsequent behavior.

Adults

Work that directly concerns separation anxiety in adults is extremely limited. This is particularly interesting given the attention to separation anxiety in children. We can conjecture that parental separation anxiety greatly influences their behavior toward their children. For example, a parent who becomes very anxious around separation might be particularly overprotective and constraining. This, in turn, likely has a large impact on the intensity and manifestation of separation anxiety in children. For example, a child who has had an overprotective parent might have an exaggerated urge to escape when separation is in the offing.

The lack of inquiry concerning adults is also surprising in view of the fact that there are many reports showing deleterious physical and psychological consequences for adults of childhood and adult separations (e.g., House et al., 1988; Tennant et al., 1981; Roy, 1985). Studying soldiers facing combat, Janis (1963) noted that fears of separation "persist in latent form in adulthood and underlie the characteristic changes in the social behavior of persons exposed to danger: they show increased interest in establishing close affiliation with any available primary group and they *seek to be reassured that the significant persons in their lives will not leave them or break preexisting affectionate ties*" [italics in original] (p. 227). Janis also observed that groups bond more tightly together for support when facing separation pressures.

Evidence about the effects of separation on adults suggests that separation anxiety plays a prominent role in adult behavior. We know that separation can have negative psychological and physical consequences as well as an impact on adult behavior in groups. To apply these lessons to mergers, acquisitions, and employee behavior in general we require a better understanding of how separation anxiety operates. In the process of building a useful theory we also need to identify factors that shape responses to separation anxiety in addition to prior experiences of separation and loss.

SEPARATION ANXIETY AT THE INDIVIDUAL LEVEL

While some authors have previously noted the importance of separation on adult behavior (Bowlby, 1975, 1988a; Schmale, 1958; Leff et al., 1970; Moberly, 1986; Krupnick & Solomon, 1987; Van Steenberg, 1988), only the most salient separations (e.g., offspring, spouse, and parent separations) have been addressed. This research concerns how less significant separations exert a profound influence on our emotions and behavior. In particular, this research explores how separations anticipated during mergers and acquisitions affect behavior.

We have seen that separation and loss produce strong behavior-influencing emotions (Bowlby, 1975, 1980, 1988a; Haley, 1980). Many of the theoretical causes of separation anxiety have been explored in previous work concerning separation and loss. Levinson (1972) and Rosenthal (1985) both reported that the instability and discontinuity in life experiences caused by loss and separation result in powerful emotional reactions. Large uncertainty about the future and the prospect of dramatic changes in relationships and routines can also contribute to increased anxiety. As discussed above, separation anxiety is further fueled by the unconscious emotional recall of prior separations and losses, many of which have traumatic qualities. With each successive separation, prior emotions are at some level recalled and relived (Bowlby, 1980; Freud, 1917; Tennant et al., 1981). Separation anxiety can be aroused by even the smallest reminders of prior separations and it can be triggered by the tiniest of signals that a separation may occur. For example, anxiety can be caused by a close friend who acts in a distant manner because that action can communicate a desire for separation and distance.

The view of separation anxiety used throughout this book is different from that defined by bereavement researchers. They generally see separation anxiety as occurring immediately after a loss. Parkes (1969) defined separation anxiety as the result of longing for the return of a lost object in the face of the reality that the object cannot return. *Here, separation anxiety is defined in part as the result of longing for an object to stay in the face of the reality that the object might leave.* This definition takes into account emotions, cognitions, and behavior that occur prior to separation. It is important to make this distinction because this research explores individual behavior and group dynamics that happen before separation.

Like all anxieties, separation anxiety is affected by historical, situational, and future factors. Individuals become anxious at the thought of separation because earlier separations are recalled, future instability implied, and because of the threat that something will be lost. Meares (1986) has suggested that the root of separation anxiety is incomplete self-boundary formation. He suggested that separation anxiety is particularly likely when one's own thoughts and behaviors are tied closely to others and not the self. Thus, when the self-boundary is called into question, separation anxiety is likely. Meares contends that when one can own her or his own feelings and thoughts and can see them as originating internally, separation anxiety is less debilitating. His work implies that separation, when managed properly, can have the positive outcome of an enhanced individual identity. Bowlby (1973a) argued that we should think of separation as having an effect simply because of separation itself. He viewed separation anxiety as a universal human reaction, regardless of individual history or context.

The above discussion indicates that separation anxiety is stimulated when an individual perceives the imminent separation of an individual or group to which he or she is attached. This can be expressed as Hypothesis 1:

Separation anxiety is stimulated in individuals by the announcement of the imminent departure of one or more group members and separation anxiety is stimulated in groups by the announced departure of one or more groups from an organization.

As a result of separation anxiety individuals exhibit certain predictable emotions and behaviors. One factor that helps explain why some behaviors are more likely than others is previous experience. People may develop characteristic ways of coping with separation. For example, some people may always feel the need to fight violently when separating.

Two other ways for predicting coping behaviors are by exploring how the behaviors prepare the individual for life following separation and how they serve to make up for relationships lost and changed as a result of separation. Consciously or unconsciously, separation anxiety prompts the modification of roles and relationships and often causes one to overlook the question: Do I want to change? In order to cope with separation many people do not actively think about how they might need to change, preferring instead to replicate relationships, search out new relationships or to strengthen existing relationships in order to replace old ones (Barry et al., 1965; Parkes, 1972). Others attempt to modify themselves in order to fill vacated roles (Bloom-Feshbach & Bloom-Feshbach, 1987). It is likely that some eventually use the energy unleashed during the separation experience for personal growth and development.

The concepts of life structure (Levinson et al., 1978) and boundary (Meares, 1986; Alderfer, 1980; Miller, 1959) are useful in understanding the specific effects of separation anxiety. Signs of impending separation alert us to the fact that our life structure is not secure and boundaries may need to change. New relationships "central to the individual" are integrated into, or removed from, the individual life structure. For example, young adults incorporate teachers, mentors, and lovers more fully into their individual life structure, as parents become less central. Life structure modification is necessary for continued development. It can also be disruptive, painful, and detrimental. A related line of research concerns the process of dying and how it affects the terminally ill. Kubler-Ross (1969) identified a sequence of coping emotions and beliefs, from denying that death would occur to its acceptance. Her studies concerned dying individuals. Others have found similar patterns for the bereaved. Jacobs et al. (1987-88) found that multiple coping mechanisms occur simultaneously, albeit with different patterns of intensity. Similar emotions are likely present in individuals who face separation.

There are certain characteristics of the individual that impact how one copes with separation anxiety. These include personal experiences, the role that the person or people separating played, plans for personal change and biologic determinants. In addition, separation anxiety always takes place within a relational context. In order to more fully understand the effects of separation anxiety we also need to consider characteristics of the relationship(s) affected by the impending separation. For the purposes of this research we will focus on the relationships that exist within a small work group. Specifically, we will examine how group process shapes and is shaped by separation anxiety. How group processes affect emotional and behavioral responses of the dying, the bereaved, and those suffering separation anxiety, have not yet been systematically studied.

SEPARATION ANXIETY AT THE GROUP LEVEL

New theory about the relationship of group process and separation anxiety is developed here because group behavior research concerning separation anxiety is sparse. Harry Levinson (1972) has shown the importance of loss for individuals in organizational life. He discussed the powerful emotions and behavioral dysfunctions that even trivial losses precipitate. In writing about large-scale organizational change, Rosenthal (1985) noted some consequences of "anticipatory mourning" prior to change. He observed that the failure to acknowledge and deal with the breaking of affectional bonds generally resulted in resistance and depressive reactions to change. Aside from brief mentions in family dynamics literature concerning death, divorce, and adolescent departure, few have dealt with the impact of separation on group behavior (cf. Bowen, 1978; McGoldrick & Walsh, 1983; Sklar & Harris, 1985; Stierlin, 1974).

Group development research also does not consider issues of separation anxiety in depth. These researchers (e.g., Kuypers et al., 1986; Gersick, 1985; Bennis & Shepard, 1956) generally discussed separation only in terms of the demise of an entire group. They did not consider how individuals and groups are affected by the imminent departure of one or more members while the rest of the group continues. Indeed, some of the phenomena which they discovered during the life cycle of groups may be closely connected with the changing level of separation anxiety in the group.

Developing theory to address the connection between the individual and group effects of separation anxiety requires an exploration of group dynamics. The concept of group boundary is particularly useful in understanding the effects of separation anxiety. During mergers and acquisitions, group boundaries are often modified as members leave and as new individuals and groups are integrated into existing groups. As well as signalling a need to restructure boundaries at the individual level, threats of separation are perceived as stressful and potentially damaging to the integrity of group boundaries. They disturb group equilibrium (cf. Ziller, 1965). They generally signal a need to restructure relationships. The question of who will remain and who might exit the group gains in importance. Who can be counted on and to what extent become issues when separation anxiety is aroused. The Three Musketeers, for example, repeatedly reaffirmed, "All for one, one for all, that is our device!" when faced with the possibility of separation.

Concepts from established theories can be employed to help explain how separation anxiety functions in relational contexts. Psychoanalytic and group dynamics literature suggests that groups facing increased anxieties due to a perceived threat attempt to cope with them through the processes of denial, splitting, and projection (Bion, 1961; Krantz, 1985; Jaques, 1974). Denial is when the sources of anxiety are disregarded or discredited. For example, denial can be seen in groups when members act as though a threat is not real or that they can keep it from happening. Denial can serve two purposes as a coping behavior. It reduces the conscious level of anxiety and can enable an otherwise paralyzed group to work. Further, this coping behavior can also raise the level of comfort and encourage people to overlook important issues. Especially likely to be disregarded are issues that indicate and predict the separation of the group. If denial raises the comfort level enough it can foster the avoidance of work.

Splitting is when good and bad qualities are identified as being dichotomous and often mutually exclusive even though in reality they cannot exist separately. For example, happy and sad are two sides of an emotion that is frequently split. Projection is when the good qualities and emotions are attributed to one individual or group (usually oneself or one's own group), while the bad qualities and emotions are attributed to another individual or group such as a scapegoat or a scapegoat group. Splitting and projection can help motivate a group. They allow group members to view the group as successful and capable of productive and useful work. However, it can also lead to arrogance and an unwillingness to cooperate. In general, during the processes of splitting and projection one or several people are excised from the group, discouraged and made powerless.

Group dynamics and coping behaviors are often determined by boundaries that exist within groups. This can readily be seen in the fact that heterogeneous groups function differently than homogenous groups. When separation anxiety is stimulated a boundary forms between members of the group who are staying and those who expect to leave. For example, group members who expect to leave may fight with staying members to remain in the group. Reactions of group members will therefore depend on whether they are on the staying or leaving side of the boundary, the degree of support they have from others on their side of the boundary, and the degree of resistance they face from across the boundary. For the purposes of this research, where all group members are assumed to have similar stature, authority, and seniority, the level of support and resistance is closely tied to the number of people on either side of the boundary.

In sum, separation anxiety exerts a powerful force on the dynamics of a group, which, in turn, greatly influences individual and group responses to separation anxiety. We now explore how different configurations of staying and leaving members affect responses to separation anxiety.

When All Members Leave a Group

Groups in which every member expects to leave (i.e., group dissolution) are likely to form a strong boundary around the group which fosters the denial of their imminent separation. In this scenario all members share the additional similarity of being asked to leave. This common characteristic increases the degree of group homogeneity. Increased bonding and a strengthening of the group boundary is facilitated by increased similarity of membership and occurs because group members seek emotional support from one another and attempt to reaffirm their attachments. Because social support can occur only after group members interact, it is expected that the activation of denial and other coping mechanisms follows a sudden and temporary increase in individual anxiety. This is represented by Hypothesis 2:

When all members leave a group: In groups where separation anxiety is stimulated and all group members share the same status of leavers, it is expected that a small increase in distress will be followed by the establishment of an insulating boundary around the entire group. As a result of the activation of denial and protective mechanisms, group members are not expected to show any additional increase in distress.

When Some Members Leave a Group While Others Stay

In many situations, some group members remain while others are expected to leave. When separation anxiety occurs in these cases, a boundary is expected to develop between those who expect to leave and those who expect to stay. Evidence of this boundary can be seen in significantly different attitudes and behavior between leaving and staying members. Remaining members are expected to have difficulty acknowledging their own feelings about separation. This occurs because remaining members seek to insulate themselves from the emotional pain of separation anxiety. Pain comes from the sources mentioned above and from the somewhat empathic realization that they could be the ones leaving. Remaining members are predisposed to seeing unpleasant and negative feelings as the domain of those leaving and to seeing their own discomfort as caused by those leaving. This places great pressure on leaving members to feel negatively. Keeping leaving members nearby provides staying members with an opportunity to avoid the intensity of their own unpleasant feelings. Likewise, leaving members garner emotional support and otherwise engage the group in order to avoid separation. This points to a paradox: Separation anxiety causes people to strengthen emotional bonds, which can make separation more distressing and emotionally wrenching. Strengthening emotional bonds further makes separation difficult because it inhibits change in general and in particular the formation of new attachments and attachments to nongroup individuals. The dynamics set in motion when some members are to leave while others are to remain lead to a more fragile group boundary while promoting the development of a strong intra-group boundary. This can be expressed as Hypothesis 3:

When one or two members leave a group while others remain: An intra-group boundary will develop in groups containing both leaving and staying members. Remaining members seek to insulate themselves from the emotional pain associated with separation while leaving members attempt to secure emotional support. The intra-group boundary is expected to be evidenced by significantly different attitudes and feelings between staying and leaving members. (cf. Alderfer, 1986; Tajfel, 1970)

The number of people that are expected to leave and remain in a group affects individual emotions and behavior, and group process. This is because the availability of emotional support increases with the number of people sharing similar position or status. Evidence supporting this view was reported by Sklar and Harris (1985). They found that family size plays a critical role in child reactions to parental loss. A greater number of siblings was associated with less severe reactions. Steinglass et al. (1985) reported that the number of family and friends available for emotional support was indicative of significantly fewer stress-related reactions for adults who underwent compulsory relocation.

The ability to sustain protective boundaries also increases with the relative number of people sharing similar position or status. A large number of remaining members can easily maintain a boundary that excludes leaving members. Likewise, the number of leaving members affects the ways they can resist exclusion and ostracism. Leaving members are better able to fight segregation as their relative number increases. In some cases, fighting serves to keep a group together. Argument often creates a forum in which communication takes place, emotions are shared, and attachments are built and reaffirmed.

The general idea that the number of leaving and remaining members is related to how separation anxiety is experienced and how it affects group process can be expressed as Hypothesis 4:

When one or two members leave a group while others remain: Group process is affected by the number of people leaving and remaining. This is seen in the evolution of differences in the experiences of staying and leaving members. Specifically, individual distress and attitudes towards the group are related to the number of people leaving and remaining. This is due to both their changing position in the group (e.g., central or peripheral) and because of group process (e.g., infighting or exclusion/withdrawal) influenced by separation anxiety.

Specific hypotheses can be developed with regard to how the number of members leaving and staying affects group process. As the number of leaving members increases, so do their opportunities to find social support, their ability to fight ostracism and separation, and their ability to deny their separation. In groups where a small minority are expected to leave, there is little opportunity for them to engender support and resist exclusion. Likewise, remaining members face fewer obstacles to projecting their negative emotions onto the leaving members and viewing emotional pain as the domain of the leaving. These dynamics are reflected in Hypothesis 4a:

When one member leaves a group while others remain: In groups where one member is expected to leave, members who are in an isolated position (e.g., one person separating a group where five are remaining) experience greater distress than remaining group members; feel more excluded even if their remaining group members report acting excessively to include them; and feel negatively about their group's work and its members. This implies that they are isolated by remaining group members. The people who stay in those same groups are expected to be more positive about their group and their emotional state. This suggests that they are denying the personal impact of the separation and are indeed rejecting their leaving members.

Many groups that face separation have a larger proportion of members who are expected to leave; for example, two members leaving a group where three are remaining. In this scenario, the number of members leaving allows them to support one another in their fight against exclusion. In these cases, the number of leaving and staying members interacting inhibits the denial and exclusion of leaving members. The conditions set up an intragroup conflict: Leaving members perceive enough support to try to counteract their exclusion and staying members are supported in their effort to draw a separate boundary around themselves. When leaving members attempt to deny their separation, staying members are quick to remind them of the group reality. Likewise, when staying members attempt to exclude those leaving, leaving members strongly resist. This situation is characterized by communication between the two sides, staying and leaving, and a general feeling of inclusion. It can be stated as Hypothesis 4b:

When two members leave a group while others remain: In groups where separation anxiety is expected to cause a boundary dividing the group into a pair who are expected to leave and a majority who are expected to remain, staying and leaving members are expected to initially experience moderately high levels of distress. After substantial interaction, members are expected to hold fairly similar views of their group and have similar emotional states. This suggests that the leaving individuals banded together to fight ostracism. Their active stance and the subsequent heightened interaction between leaving and staying group members fosters a shared view and greater bonding within the group.

There are a number of other possible scenarios in which some members of a group are expected to leave while others remain; for example, situations in which a majority of the group is expected to leave while a minority are expected to stay. Because of efforts to keep the scope of this research narrow and because of the strong interest of the author in situations in which a minority of the group is expected to separate, the many other alternative situations in which some members of the group are expected to leave while others remain were not explored.

When All Members Stay in a Group While Others in Their Organization Leave

Another situation occurs when all members are expected to stay, yet separation anxiety has been stimulated. For example, this happens when group members learn that while they are not expected to leave, other people in their organization will leave. In such situations, members feel relatively secure and therefore feel little need to deny the separation of others. They can project their anxiety onto leaving members and can discuss pain and anger which they perceive as feelings belonging to leaving members. Rather than fostering strong denial, it is expected that this situation will promote somewhat open discussion. This is Hypothesis 5:

When all members stay in a group while others in their organization are expected to leave: In groups where separation anxiety is stimulated yet all group members are expected to stay (e.g., others in their organization are expected to leave), members are expected to have relatively uninhibited discussion. This suggests that members within the group identify with the remaining and leaving members of their organization. Both sides of the issue, leaving and remaining, can be discussed within the group.

SUMMARY

There is abundant evidence that separation anxiety is an important issue and has profound effects for individuals and groups. The roots of separation anxiety are believed to be established during the earliest phases of life and it is a phenomenon that is not limited to our species. The theory proposed here indicates that separation anxiety will be stimulated in groups facing the impending separation of one or more of its members or of other members within their organization. Further, the inclusion of group dynamics concepts in the theory leads to the prediction that the number of members leaving and remaining in a group strongly affects individual and group responses to separation anxiety.

With the theoretical groundwork laid out and specific hypotheses generated, Chapter 3 addresses the method used to empirically investigate the theory and test the hypotheses.

3

Creating a Simulation of Mergers and Acquisitions

Mergers and acquisitions provide a fertile setting for the study of separation anxiety. As noted in Chapter 1, mergers and acquisitions often produce separation anxiety because of the likelihood of dramatic organizational changes including layoffs, transfers, and reorganizations. It is estimated that there were over 5,000 mergers and acquisitions in 1988 (*Forbes*, 1988). Harshbarger (1987) reported that between 1981 and 1986, well over 500,000 executives lost jobs as the result of mergers and acquisitions. These figures would be much larger if they included privately owned and governmental organizations.

To begin answering the questions, "How do mergers and acquisitions raise employee anxiety and how, in turn, does this anxiety affect behavior, satisfaction, productivity, and effectiveness?", a mergers and acquisitions simulation was created. Specifically, the simulation was designed to explore: (1) whether or not separation anxiety is stimulated by the anticipated exit of group member(s); (2) whether or not separation anxiety is stimulated by the anticipated exit of groups in an organization; (3) how individual and group responses to separation anxiety are mediated by the number of group members leaving; and (4) how individual and group experiences of separation anxiety are influenced by whether or not the individual anticipates leaving or staying in the group.

Questionnaires were developed to measure group process, group attitudes, and individual emotional state. The analytical design, which is discussed later, used a repeated measures (Winer, 1962) and an after-only design. To increase reliability, the research design included three runs of the simulation, yielding two replications.

The simulation was designed to be both an exercise for the collection of data as well as a learning experience for simulation participants. A further feature of the design was that it solicited personal experiences from participants in order to further their learning as well as to gather information which was not directly related to the simulation experience. All participants were taking a course that concerned individual behavior in organizations.

SIMULATION DESIGN OVERVIEW

This 90-minute simulation placed individuals in groups of five to six members. As shown in Figure 1, the simulation consisted of five components: (1) introduction; (2) group formation; (3) psychological contracting; (4) members learn who is leaving; and (5) group task. The simulation varied the number of people separating and remaining in small groups according to five conditions: (1) Control group—no separation information was given; (2) Others Leave group—the group was told that all group members would stay while others in the organization would to leave; (3) All Leave group—all members of the group were to leave; (4) One Leaves group—one specific person was to leave; and (5) Two Leave group—two specific members were to leave. The last two groups had departing and remaining members. For analytic purposes, to be discussed in more depth later, each of the last two groups were partitioned into staying and leaving members in order to examine their different experiences.

After being assigned to groups, each group was then given their own room in order to promote the development of a shared group boundary (Miller, 1959). The first activity was an attachment-building exercise adapted from the psychological contracting model provided by Kotter (1973). In order to stimulate separation anxiety attachments needed to be nurtured. This was particularly important because many participants had never worked together before and did not have on-going relationships.

After the attachment-building period, participants were given a company history and a current event document. The company history document was written to promote the feeling of attachment to the work group and the organization. It stated things such as: you are part of an established and well-respected multidivisional company that has very low turnover; you are part of a senior human-resources policy-making group, members generally only leave this group when they retire or are promoted to a divisional presidency; and that you and other members hold this group to be the most import group belonged to, both professionally and socially; this group is second only to your families in importance.

The current event document, which was composed from real-life events, set the stage for the merger. It was designed to first reinforce individual and group attachments and to then introduce the notion that a group member(s) would be asked to leave. This document delivered the primary experimental

Figure 1
Simulation Design

Group Conditions	Control [no merger indicated]	Others Leave [entire group stays, but others in organization will leave]	All Leave [entire group told all will leave]	One Leaves [group told one member will leave]	Two Leave [group told two members will leave]
Period 1: Introduction [before exercise begins]					
Period 2: Group Formation [participants learn who is in each group]					
Period 3: Psychological Contracting [group members form attachments]					
Period 4: Leavers Become Known [members learn about company background, current events, and who will be leaving]					
Period 5: Group Task [group members determine best questions to ask of CEOs of either or both firms]					

manipulation of the simulation: it stated how many people would be asked to leave the group and whether or not the reader would be asked to leave.

After learning who was to leave the group and organization, the groups performed a merger-related task. The task was to have the group discuss and choose three questions from a list to ask either the Chief Executive Officer (CEO) of their organization and/or the CEO of the merging company. The simulation ended at the close of the task period.

Two days later, all participants attended a 90-minute simulation debriefing session. Further discussion of the simulation and of separation anxiety in general occurred during a 90-minute session which took place five days after the first debriefing session.

SIMULATION SETTING AND PARTICIPANTS

The simulation occurred as a learning exercise in two different courses: one in organizational behavior at Yale University and one in human-resources management at Michigan State University. The differences between the courses and students added robustness to the experiment. The simulation occurred three times. The participants of two runs were undergraduates in an introductory organizational behavior course at Yale University. The participants of one run were masters students in an introductory human-resources course at Michigan State University. Having two replications also added a check on the stability of the findings.

While the contents of the courses were different, the design of the undergraduate and masters courses began with issues of attachment and "joining-up" and ended with issues of termination, separation, and loss. In both settings, the simulation was run and debriefed during the latter part of the semester.

The Yale Course

The researcher, a White male, was the teaching fellow and coauthor of the courses taught at Yale University. The senior faculty member, a Black male, was a lecturer in organizational behavior. Topics covered in the course included attachment theory; adult psychosocial development; the effects of gender, race, and social class on behavior, group, and intergroup dynamics; and separation and loss.

The course was an experiential course based on exercises designed to stimulate self-reflection. Several were highly evocative, including an exercise in which one-third of the class purposely oppressed two-thirds of the class for a full class session. Because the course involved a high degree of self-disclosure and emotionality, students and staff felt quite close to one another by the end of the term.

Faculty developed significant relationships with the students, both in the classroom and during optional personal interviews. The faculty fostered an open and emotionally accessible environment in the classroom by encouraging students to examine their relationships with members of the class in a nonevaluative manner. The faculty repeatedly announced that they would be available after class sessions ended and after the course was completed. Indeed, many students requested and received help regarding issues discussed in class and several students wrote letters to the faculty concerning their experiences after graduation. One student arranged for the faculty to give a race-relations and cultural-diversity workshop to a group of Yale freshmen and women.

The Michigan State Course

The masters class at Michigan State University was given by a White female colleague of the author. At that time, she was an assistant professor in the School of Industrial and Labor Relations. The researcher went to Michigan State University for four days to lead two class sessions that included the simulation and one debriefing session. While the masters class was a more traditional human-resources management course and was less concerned with the discussion of emotions, it included small-group work and promoted self-reflection. The professor of this course also established close relationships, involving mutual trust, with her students. The author's entry into the class and the establishment of a trusting environment was facilitated by the close relationships of the researcher and the professor and the professor and her students. The professor has used a slightly modified version of the simulation as a learning exercise in her subsequent classes.

Confidentiality

At the beginning of the courses, faculty discussed with students the possibility of using experiences in the class to refine the courses and to help others learn in the future. There was an agreement with the class such that if any student requested their experiences to be excluded in future class materials or other public work, their requests would be honored. Students were told that all information was to be kept confidential and that identities of class members would be kept anonymous in any reports of class activities. While students of the Yale course were told that their experiences would likely be used in future publications, students in the Michigan State course were explicitly told that their work would be part of the author's research.

Number of Participants

A total of 23 groups (N = 119) were included in this research. Because of the number of participants, only the first run included all five experimental conditions (Control, Others Leave, All Leave, Two Leave and One Leaves groups). The choice of the number of groups run for each condition was made in order to increase the number of leaving individuals in the One Leaves and

Table 1
Number of Participants Per Condition by Setting*

Group	Undergraduates Yale University 1987	Masters Michigan State University 1987	Undergraduates Yale University 1988	Total Sample Size
Control	12 (2)	0 (0)	4 (4)	16 (3)
All Leave	10 (2)	5 (1)	0 (0)	15 (3)
Others Leave	11 (2)	0 (0)	0 (0)	11 (2)
One Leaves	10 (2)	15 (3)	20 (4)	45 (9)
Leaving	2	3	4	9
Staying	8	12	16	36
Two Leave	12 (2)	10 (2)	10 (2)	32 (6)
Leaving	4	4	4	12
Staying	8	6	6	20
Total	**55 (10)**	**30 (6)**	**34 (7)**	**119 (23)**

* Number of groups per condition in parentheses.

Two Leave groups: The 9 One Leaves groups resulted in 9 individual leaving members and 36 staying members, and the 6 Two Leave groups resulted in 12 leaving members and 20 staying members. The number of participants in each group is given in Table 1.

DATA COLLECTION INSTRUMENTS

Two quantitative instruments were used to collect data. Prior to the simulation, a transitions distress questionnaire was administered to gauge the stress participants associated with 20 common transitions. A repeated measures questionnaire was designed to measure attitudes towards the groups, group process, and individual emotional state before, during, and after the simulation. The questionnaire given at the end of the simulation also included after-only questions which were designed to measure group process and the degree to which separation was recognized as an issue for the groups. Qualitative data were also collected including observations of the simulation and debriefing sessions and a term paper written by each participant.

Transitions Distress Questionnaire

Three weeks prior to the simulation, participants filled out a

Exhibit 1
Sample from Transitions Distress Questionnaire

In the left-hand blank beside each transition below, please indicate the number of times you have had each transition and the date of the latest one. **Whether or not you have experienced them, on the scale underneath each question please circle the number which corresponds to how emotionally stressful each category of transition is for you.** Stress refers to the immediate and lasting effects of a category of transition. When judging the stress of past transitions, be sure to also reflect upon seemingly dissociated events that occurred shortly before, during and shortly after the transition. Note: Family of origin refers to the family you were born into, family of creation refers to the family that you create.

Number of   Date of Most
Transitions   Recent Transition (Year)

___   ___   Marriage(s).

0	1	2	3	4
Question does not apply	Very Stressful	Somewhat Stressful	Slightly Stressful	Not at all Stressful

questionnaire that measured stress associated with 20 specific transitions. The questionnaire consisted of 20 four-point items. Participants indicated how stressful they regarded each of the 20 common transitions, whether or not they had actually experienced the particular transition. This questionnaire was used to make group assignments and to provide a check on the relationship between transition distress and separation anxiety experienced during the simulation.

Transitions in this questionnaire included deaths of parents, siblings, friends, and spouse; geographical relocations; marriages; births; and divorces. Exhibit 1 is a sample from this questionnaire. The entire questionnaire is reproduced in Appendix 1.

Repeated Measures Questionnaire

In order to gauge member experiences during the simulation a two-part questionnaire was constructed. The questionnaire was given after each of the five periods in order to provide repeated measures for the repeated measures analysis. The first part of the questionnaire consisted of 11 six-point items that measured individual views of the group. The choice of a six-point scale reflected the philosophical belief that perfect neutrality on an agree-disagree scale is not theoretically possible. An example from this questionnaire is provided in Exhibit 2. The entire questionnaire is reproduced in Appendix 2.

Exhibit 2
Sample from Group Views Section of Simulation Questionnaire

Please circle the response which best characterizes your reaction to the following statements.

The quality of my group's work will be the best compared to all others.

1	2	3	4	5	6
Agree	Agree Somewhat	Agree Slightly	Disagree Slightly	Disagree Somewhat	Disagree

The issues that this section of the questionnaire were designed to examine concerned group characteristics and were as follows:

1. Like Group.
   I like my group a great deal.

2. Quality of group work.
   The quality of my group's work is the best compared to all others.

3. Individual contribution to group.
   I have made a large contribution to my group's work.

4. Understanding.
   I am understood by my group's members.
   I understand my group's members.

5. Openness.
   My group's members are open to my suggestions.
   I am open to the suggestions of my group's members.

6. Group enhances and detracts from individual ability to work.
   The group enhances my ability to work.
   The group detracts from my ability to work.

7. Inclusion and exclusion.
   I have a great sense of "feeling included" in my group.
   I feel left out of my group.

The second half of the questionnaire contained 20 five-point items that took an inventory of current emotional state. A sample question is provided in Exhibit 3.

The items designed to assess individual current emotional state included the following mixture of negative and positive emotions.

1. Negative Emotions.
   Afraid

Angry
Anxious
Depressed
Jittery
Lonely
Nervous
On Edge
Sad
Tense

2.   Positive Emotions.
Calm
Carefree
Comfortable
Confident
Content
Happy
Pleased
Safe
Secure
Sure of Self

After-Only Questions

Additional questions were integrated into the questionnaire given after the fifth period of the exercise to provide post-simulation measures of group process for the after-only analysis. These were 16 six-point questions that were designed to reveal intragroup interactions and group processes. Exhibit 4 displays a sample from this questionnaire. The entire questionnaire given after the fifth period is reproduced in Appendix 3.   The group-related issues addressed in the post-simulation portion of the questionnaire were as follows:

1.   Group Boundary.
I had the feeling of being closer to my group members after the simulation ended than I did before it began.
My group chose the best questions from the list.
I was angry with my group.

2.   Separation Was an Issue for the Group.
I believe that one of the primary underlying issues that we were dealing with and that influenced our behavior was group separation.
I believe that one of the primary underlying issues that we were dealing with and that influenced our behavior was individual separation.

Exhibit 3
Sample from Current Emotions Section of Simulation Questionnaire

> Below you will find descriptive words that refer to emotions. Please circle the number which best represents your current emotional state.
>
> | Afraid | 1 | 2 | 3 | 4 | 5 |
> |--------|------|----------|----------|----------|------------|
> | | Very | Somewhat | Slightly | A Little | Not at All |

Exhibit 4
Sample from Additional Group Process Questions

> I believe that one of the primary underlying issues that we were dealing with and that influenced our behavior was individual separation.
>
> | 1 | 2 | 3 | 4 | 5 | 6 |
> |-------|----------|----------|----------|----------|----------|
> | Agree | Agree | Agree | Disagree | Disagree | Disagree |
> | | Somewhat | Slightly | Slightly | Somewhat | |

3. Individuals Being Isolated and Formation of Alliances.

   There was one member of our group who would probably be identified unanimously as our group's leader.

   I had not a single strong alliance with any member of my group during the task discussion.

   There were two members of my group who were unfairly trying to influence the group for their own benefit.

   I teamed up with one group member in particular during the task discussion.

   I participated more than all the other group members.

   Without me, the group would have chosen some significantly different questions.

   We chose one question to satisfy a leaving group member(s).

   After we chose a question to satisfy a leaving group member(s), we concentrated on the more important work of the task.

   The majority of the group did not want to discuss issues concerning a leaving group member(s).

   I wanted to discuss issues concerning a leaving group member(s) far more than the rest of my group did.

4. Projection onto Authority.

   I am happy with the superiors in our company—United Composite Incorporated (UCI).

These questions were given only after the simulation was over because the content of the questions had the potential to interfere with group process. The intent was to avoid asking questions which might suggest specific behaviors or important issues that were expected to arise during the simulation so that they could develop naturally.

Qualitative Data Collection

Two other sources of data were collected: observations of the simulation and debriefing periods, and term papers and homework assignments required of all participants. Exhibit 5 shows the homework assignment which was designed to get a brief description of why the group selected the questions it chose during the task segment of the exercise.

The term paper assignment was designed to cover the entire course and is displayed in Exhibit 6. The assignment was designed to be an educational exercise in which students were to synthesize and expand on their learning over the entire course. The term paper assignment was very open-ended so that the discussion of the simulation and separation anxiety was not forced, but was allowed to emerge if students felt these topics were important. It was expected that this would enable a more in-depth discussion, encourage the generation of new data not from the course, and allow the more transferential learnings to emerge. The term papers were included in this research to provide a richness of data that is not obtainable through multiple-choice questionnaire responses. Again, regarding confidentiality, students were told that their work might be included in future publications. They were also given the option of asking to not have their work made public. Several students requested not to have their papers included in future work in any way and their requests were honored.

Hypotheses and Questionnaire Instruments

The questionnaires were designed to fulfill dual purposes: to provide data for both hypothesis testing and exploratory research. It was anticipated that exploratory information could be interpreted apart from the hypotheses.

It was expected that Control group members would report a constant level of all the variables examined in the questionnaire, demonstrating that they were unaffected by separation anxiety. For all other conditions it was expected that the simulation would result in the stimulation of separation anxiety that would be evidenced in reports of negative affect after participants learned that separations were going to occur in their organization or group.

In the All Leave groups, where the entire group was to leave, it was expected that following the announcement that they would all be leaving, there

Exhibit 5
Homework Assignment for Merger and Acquisition Simulation

Before you gain too much distance from this simulation, write down the reasons for why you chose the questions that you chose and why your group ended up choosing the questions it chose. You do not have to be analytical in your answer. Be straightforward and give the reasons as you thought about them and as your group discussed them. You might also want to write down any thoughts, recollections, etc. that will come in useful in later discussions or in the final paper.

would be an initial period of increased liking of the group, reflecting the activation of social support needs and the drawing of a close boundary. This period was expected to be followed by a decrease in liking of the group as the boundary became too confining and members attempted to ease the separation by disliking one another. This does not necessarily mean that they were expected to openly communicate growing mutual dislike. Their heightened boundary was also expected to induce them to positively experience a high

Exhibit 6
Final Paper Assignment

This is an introspective assignment. The topic on which you should write is as follows:

Take this paper as an opportunity to synthesize what has happened for you this semester during the course. Think about the dynamic relationship between individual behavior and group membership. Consider how you have influenced and have been influenced by our class experiences and other group and intergroup situations. Examine how your multiple group memberships have affected your behavior during the course.

In preparing the paper, class members should select and incorporate those concepts and theories (formal and informal) that they personally find most useful in understanding what they describe. We do not expect people to employ the readings mechanically or by rote. We do encourage people to criticize and refine concepts which they feel are limited. **Remember to support your analyses with data.**

Writing this paper will provide an opportunity to practice effective written communications. The ability to accurately and clearly articulate your thoughts is crucial. The editorial and grammatical character of the paper refers both to the overall logic of the paper and to the structure of individual sentences and paragraphs. Our jobs are made easier if the paper is well written and clearly thought through. You may know what you're talking about, however, if you fail to communicate effectively we will not know what you're talking about and as a result, your grade will suffer.

This final term paper should be no less than twenty pages nor longer than thirty pages. We expect papers to be easily readable. Light dot matrix printing and triple spacing are unacceptable. Papers should have easily readable print and double spacing only. Papers are to be an individual effort.

Individuals may consult with the staff in advance of the due date.

level of inclusion in the group and group process. Prior to their interaction, it was expected that the stimulation of separation anxiety would result in an initial negative change in affect. The subsequent denial of separation was anticipated to be revealed in a generally good emotional state. Demonstrating that no internal boundaries had developed, it was expected that All Leave group members would report that a leader did not emerge in the group, that there was little alliance formation, and that everyone felt included in the group.

In the Others Leave groups, where everyone in the group was to stay but others in the organization were to leave, it was expected that there would be a steady or slightly increasing level of liking of the group, reflecting their slightly increased boundary strength resulting from the moderate stimulation of separation anxiety. No indication of intragroup boundary formation such as a leader emerging or alliances forming was expected.

In the One Leaves and Two Leave groups its was expected that there would be differences in the experiences of the staying and leaving members. In the One Leaves groups, it was expected that leaving members would increasingly dislike their groups as a result of their being isolated. The leaving members of the One Leave groups were expected to show a negative affective trend in general. It was anticipated that they would feel increasingly sad, tense, and so on. Being isolated and without opportunities for social support, it was also anticipated that they would increasingly experience the group process as being flawed. The after-only items were expected to reveal that they did not form alliances, participated little, were angry with their superiors, thought that their group did not choose the best questions during the task, and wanted to discuss issues concerning the leaving member far more than did the staying members.

The staying members of the One Leaves groups were expected to increasingly like their group as a result of the formation of a new boundary around the staying members which was not resisted by the leaving member. Their liking of the group and their generally good affective state were expected to increase as a result of their projection of negative feelings onto the leaving member and onto their superiors. Evidence of their active isolation of the leaving member was expected to be seen in reports that they had chosen a question to satisfy the leaving member and then moved on to the more important work of the task.

In the Two Leave groups, it was expected that the leaving members would feel an initial period of general negative affect and dislike for their group. This would occur before any interaction took place that could lead to their forming an alliance. In general, it was expected that initially they would be negatively affected. After joining forces to resist exclusion, it was expected that their interaction with the remaining group members would lead to a positive change in affect. The leaving members' responses to the after-only questionnaire items were expected to show that alliances did form within the group and, as a result of their active efforts to remain included in the group, that they felt closer to their group after the simulation ended.

The staying members of the Two Leave groups were expected to display an increased liking of their group as they interacted in a meaningful way with leaving members. In general, it was expected that the intensity of their discussion with leaving members would lead to positive reports of affect and group process. The responses of staying members of the Two Leave groups to the after-only questionnaire items were anticipated to show that alliances formed within the group and that they felt closer to their group after the simulation ended. It is important to note that the simulation was designed to somewhat force members to interact as they were directed to meet as a group. In other circumstances, for example where the group is not given any directions after being informed of a merger, we might expect different behavior. Figure 2 displays the general hypotheses.

Simulation in Detail

Upon arrival, participants were told, "Today we will be engaged in a mergers and acquisitions simulation. We're on a tight schedule today so let's get started." They were then given the first repeated measures questionnaire. Participants identified themselves by name on the questionnaires. The first questionnaire was given to familiarize participants with the instrument and to gain a measure for the repeated measures analysis of variance.

Group assignments were announced after the questionnaires were collected. The transitions distress questionnaire results were used to divide participants into three categories: high-, medium-, and low-transition distress. Simulation groups had equivalent numbers of randomly assigned people from each stress category. Placing all the high distress participants together was avoided. Groups were assigned their own secluded work space in order to aid the process of attachment and group boundary formation.

The first packet was distributed after participants arrived at their locations. Packets were color coded by group to insure proper data processing and to provide groups with an additional boundary symbol. The first packet contained a second questionnaire and a psychological contracting exercise. The questionnaire was given before the contracting exercise. The second questionnaire was given to gain a measure for the repeated measures analysis of variance and to gauge the affects of participants' knowing who would be in their groups.

The psychological contracting exercise, shown in Exhibit 7, encouraged the formation of attachments among group members. The exercise was a modified version of one presented by Kotter (1973). In the 20 minutes allotted, group members constructed a contract that included items such as shared hopes and fears, expectations of commitment to the group and its work,

Figure 2
General Hypotheses

Group Conditions	Control [no merger indicated]	Others Leave [entire group stays, but others in organization will leave]	All Leave [entire group told all will leave]	One Leaves [group told one member will leave]	Two Leave [group told two members will leave]
Period 1: Introduction [before exercise begins]	Preseparation anxiety stimulation: No hypotheses. Participants told this is a simulation. Period concerns familiarization with questionnaire instrument.				
Period 2: Group Formation [participants learn who is in each group]	Preseparation anxiety stimulation: No hypotheses. Period concerns the beginning of attachment process.				
Period 3: Psychological Contracting [group members form attachments]	Preseparation anxiety stimulation: No hypotheses. Groups have formed and attachments have been established.				
Period 4: Leavers Become Known [members learn about company background, current events, and who will be leaving]	No significant changes.	Small negative change.	Small-to-moderate negative change.	Leavers: large negative change. Stayers: small negative change.	Leavers: large negative change. Stayers: small negative change.
Period 5: Group Task [group members determine best questions to ask of CEOs of either or both firms]	No significant changes.	Small positive change.	Large positive change.	Leavers: large negative change. Stayers: small positive change.	Leavers: large positive change. Stayers: small positive change.

and degree of honesty and confidentiality required by the group. Group members presented, discussed, compromised, and finally agreed on items included in the document. All participants had previously taken part in a similar exercise. This period of attachment building was included in order to increase the likelihood that separation anxiety would be stimulated by the

Exhibit 7
Group Formation Task

> For the next fifteen minutes your group is to get to know one another. Begin the process of "Psychological Contracting." Using a regular sheet of paper, write up your group's initial contract. Items that you may wish to cover are hopes and fears, commitment, honesty, and confidentiality. *Be sure to include each member's name on the sheet of paper.*

announcement that a member(s) would be leaving the group.

After the group formation exercise, participants received the second packet. This packet contained five items to be read and completed in order: a third questionnaire, company history, current event, group task, and fourth questionnaire. The color coding of this packet contained further symbolic information. The randomly chosen leaving members received pink colored packets. "Pink sheets" are commonly associated with layoffs and firings. The third questionnaire measured attitudes and feelings after attachment building. Leaving members had not yet been asked to leave at the time they took the third questionnaire.

After completing the questionnaire, participants read the remaining documents. The company history, displayed in Exhibit 8, indicated that the company had a tradition of no mergers, acquisitions, or layoffs. Turnover and transfers were very low. Group members learned that they were part of a senior human-resources policy group and that members were very involved, attached, and committed to their group. This document was provided to give participants background information and to reinforce the attachments that they had established.

The subsequent document, the current event document, contained the primary manipulation. Two lines, in bold face, indicated the individual's disposition. Except for the control group, this document stated that the company was merging with a competitor and decisions about who would leave were final. Control group members were told only that there was a rising number of mergers and acquisitions in general. A sample of the current event document is provided in Exhibit 9.

After reading of the current event, participants examined the group task. The group task, shown in Exhibit 10, instructed the group to select from an attached list three questions which they felt the employees of the company would most like to have answered by the chairmen of their company and of the merging company. The questions were designed to have varying levels of relevance to separating and remaining members. They dealt with a range of issues including the organization after the merger, the current leaving employees, the security of remaining employees, and corporate-community relations. Control group questions were related to mergers in general.

Exhibit 8
United Composite Incorporated: Company History

Your company has been operating for over fifty years in a moderate growth industry. United Composite Incorporated (UCI) is medium sized (less than 2,000 employees) and has a multidivisional structure coordinated by a central corporate headquarters. The company has a history of starting all of its operations from scratch and never closing or divesting its operations. Employees, especially management, have generally stayed with the company in the community in which they were hired until retirement. Few request transfers and even less leave of their own choosing. UCI has a strong team spirit which originated with its founding during the Great Depression.

Your work group, located within headquarters for over fifteen years, is responsible for human resources, managerial development and related policies. Promotions come infrequently at your level in the organization. In general, there has been little turnover in the group. Generally, members only leave when they accept promotion to a divisional presidency or when they retire.

You are highly involved in your work group. Its importance in your life is second only to your family. You are very attached to your work group. During your career you have made substantial investments of time and energy into both individual group members and the work group as a whole. The prevailing feeling among group members is that this is the most important group belonged to, both professionally and socially.

Participants had 45 minutes to complete the group task. Immediately after reading the group task, participants responded to the fourth questionnaire. It measured the short term effects of the separation announcements. After replying to the questionnaire, groups had approximately 45 minutes to complete the task.

Prior to the end of the 90-minute session participants were given the final packet. It contained a fifth questionnaire and the brief homework assignment depicted in Exhibit 5. The questionnaire measured the effects of the simulation and resultant group process. In addition, as discussed above, it contained items designed to assess group process. The homework assignment asked participants to state which questions they individually chose, which ones their group chose, and the rationale for their selections.

The first debriefing session occurred two days later. During the first 45 minutes, participants met in small groups to discuss their experiences. Groups were composed of people who had the same status. That is to say, leaving members of the One Leaves groups met together, staying members of the One Leaves groups met together, leaving members of the Two Leave groups met together, and so on. This was done so that members could compare their experiences and be better able to participate in a cross-group discussion. The maximum size of these groups was eight members. During the second 45 minutes, the groups convened and individuals shared their experiences.

Exhibit 9
The Current Event

Today is Tuesday. Like your co-workers, you left early on Thursday to get a good start on your four day holiday weekend. When you returned to work this morning you could sense that something was up. There was an atmosphere of tension and suspense. Late in the morning, at least you remember it as having been late in the morning, you received a call from a credible source that the corporate chairman, the president, and board of directors approved a merger between United Composite and one of its fast growth competitors. You were told that while nothing was certain yet, the new company would likely form within sixty days.

You have been a member of the organization for well over five years and a member of your work group for over three years. Most of the other members of the work group have been there as long as you. You view yourself as having more in common with your work group than with the rest of your organization. Like other members in your work group, you perceived the merger news as a complete surprise.

Your source of information appeared to gain credibility because an hour after the phone call the building's public address system was used for the first time that you could remember. The announcement stated:

This announcement is to put substance into the rumors which seem to have been running rampant all morning. Your chairman, president, and board of directors have approved a merger with one of our chief competitors: Streamline Company. The new company will be called United Streamline Incorporated (USI). We expect the merger to be consummated in sixty days. More detailed announcements will be forthcoming.

While you were beginning to wonder what might be in the future announcements, your source called again. This time you were informed that your work group would be asked to work on a merger-related task in the near future.

You were also told that the merger would, of course, entail a reduction in combined employment and that **one member of your group will be asked to leave.**

With a bit of hesitation, your source said, "I didn't want to be the one to tell you this, but since we're, uh, close . . . It seems very likely that within thirty days or so **you will be asked to leave.**" When you asked if other members of your group know this, the answer was that they did.

Still a bit shocked, you were also informed that this decision was final and that it was highly unlikely that you would ever be able to rejoin the company.

The second debriefing session occurred five days later. For the first 45 minutes of this exercise participants met in small groups and discussed their separation experiences and the effects of separation anxiety on their lives. The small groups were formed based on the self-reported personal importance of separation anxiety. People who believed separation anxiety to be highly important met in one group, those who felt it moderately important met in another group, and so on. The maximum size of these groups was eight members. The second 45 minutes involved a large group discussion in which participants shared their experiences. The time between the simulation and the

Exhibit 10
Group Task

Your work group has been asked by the corporation's board of directors to work on an important assignment. You have been given the attached list of possible questions to ask either your current chief executive officer (CEO), the CEO of Streamline Company, or both people. Your group should select the three questions from the attached list which you believe would be most important to have answered for the entire corporation. You are to assume that if the board of directors agrees with your selections that they will indeed be asked, answered honestly, and the answers distributed throughout the organization. Your group may decide to create a question to be asked in addition to the ones selected from the list.

Before beginning group discussion, please examine the below questions. Following the group's discussion, please use a separate piece of paper and indicate the question numbers, who your group would like them asked of, and the order of priority in which the questions should be asked. Include group members' names on the paper. *Please note that if you wish to ask the same question to both people that counts as two questions.*

Questions:
1. What is our organization's primary long term goal?
2. Will there be any changes in our pay system in the near future?
3. Will there be any changes in the nature of supervisor-subordinate relationships in our company?
4. What could be done to keep changes from taking place?
5. Will there be any changes in our benefits and pension plans in the near future?
6. Will community involvement and benefit programs be eliminated in the near future?
7. Will training and development programs be eliminated in the near future?
8. Aside from those which may already have been announced, will there be any changes in the way in which individual work groups function?
9. What are the two single most important reasons for and against the merger?
10. Will our organization continue its strong emphasis on human relations and morale?
11. Is there any way for work groups to continue to keep people who are dispensable?
12. Will there be any changes in our stock option plan in the near future?
13. What is our company's estimated profits for the next four quarters?
14. How have our recent past operations influenced your decisions about change?
15. Will there be any changes in our group-based bonus system in the near future?
16. What efforts will be made to retrain people who leave the company before normal retirement age?
17. Should we have new manuals of standard operating procedures for all departments?
18. Is there any way for dispensable people to remain in the company?
19. Will we change or reduce our generous early retirement program in any way in the near future?

Exhibit 10 (Cont'd.)

20. Will the formal structure of our organization become more centralized or will we keep our operations independent and autonomous?
21. Will there be any changes in our individually based bonus system in the near future?
22. What support will be given to people who leave our company?
23. What new programs will be created to train people and otherwise benefit individual career development within our company?
24. Will there be any departments or functional units that will be eliminated in the near future?
25. Will any of our operations be liquidated or divested in the near future?
26. What plans are being made with regard to out placement for people who leave our company?
27. What new community involvement and benefit programs will be created in the near future?

debriefing sessions was determined by the class schedule. Having the debriefing sessions occur more than a day after the simulation was also expected to provide participants with time to gain distance from the experience and time for personal reflection.

Participants handed in their term papers approximately four weeks later.

SIMULATION ANALYSIS DESIGN

Scales were constructed to facilitate statistical examination of the simulation data. It was expected that two reliable scales could be constructed to represent each part of the repeated measures questionnaire: attitudes toward the group and individual emotional state. It was also anticipated that at least one reliable scale could be constructed from the transitions distress questionnaire. The scales were based on an oblique principal-components cluster analysis and were corroborated by interitem correlations. They were then used to analyze the results. In addition, several items were used for illustrative purposes. The after-only items were examined individually.

To determine the effects of the simulation, six quantitative analyses of the measures of attitudes toward the group and individual emotional state were performed. The first five analyses employ a repeated measures analysis of variance (Winer, 1962) based on the model:

scale = intercept + Period + Analytical Condition + Period*Analytical + Condition + error.[1]

For groups which had only staying or leaving members, group and analytical conditions were the same. In order to assess the differences between staying and leaving members, the One and Two Leave groups were partitioned for analytical purposes. Together, the One and Two Leave groups represented four Analytical Conditions: One Leaves members who were to stay, One Leaves members who were to leave, Two Leave members who were to stay, and Two Leave members who were to leave. Figure 3 outlines the analysis design for the repeated measures analysis of variance. Because each individual was measured before, during, and after the simulation, the repeated measures design has the advantage of providing control over individual differences within analytical conditions. In a sense, each participant served as his or her own matched control. The design also contained a second source of control. The inclusion of a control group in the experimental design served as a check on the influence of unintended effects. If the control group experiences were similar to other groups then it would be likely that something other than separation anxiety accounted for those effects.

The assumption of statistical independence of measures is an important issue in analytic designs that use each individual as his or her own control. This assumption was checked with an orthogonal components sphericity test using Mauchly's criteria (Huynh & Feldt, 1970) and with multiple analyses of variance tests.

The first analysis examined the main effect for Analytical Condition in the above model. A significant main effect would indicate that the simulation had an overall impact and that separation anxiety was stimulated. The second analysis used the interaction effect of the repeated measures analysis of variance. A significant interaction effect would indicate that the simulation had an impact and that there were differences between Analytical Conditions. In other words, the interaction effect would show that on average experiences were different depending on the group to which participants belonged.

The third analysis examines the specific impact of each Analytical Condition using a multiple analyses of variance contrast test between Periods within Analytical Conditions. This test is able to indicate if there were differences between Analytical Conditions across each of the Periods. For example, this test might show that right after the current event sheet was read participant experiences were different depending on the group to which they belonged. In conjunction with this analysis, further interpretations regarding group process were made by examining the patterns of the means. The scale means and several item means from items included within the scales were charted in order to explore the progression of differences between Analytical Conditions. For example, the Two Leave group was expected to show diverging and then converging means as leaving and staying members formed boundaries which allowed for communication across the boundary.

A fourth analysis was performed to assess the effects of separation anxiety on the various Analytical Conditions. This analysis explored the Period effects experienced by the Control group, as well as a comparison of the Period effects experienced by the Control group versus all other Analytical

Figure 3
Simulation Analysis Design

Analytical Condition (P)*			Period 1: [before exercise began]	Period 2: [after they found out who is in each group]	Period 3: [after Psychological Contracting exercise]	Period 4: [after they knew who would be asked to leave]	Period 5: [after simulation ended]
Group	G	P					
1 Control	G_1	P_1					
	.	P_2					
	.	.					
	G_n	P_n					
2 All Leave	G_1	P_1					
	.	P_2					
	.	.					
	G_n	P_n					
3 Others Leave	G_1	P_1					
	.	P_2					
	.	.					
	G_n	P_n					
4 Two Leave	G_1	P_{1leave}					
	.	P_{2leave}					
	.	P_{1stay}					
	.	.					
	G_n	$P_{n\text{-}stay}$					
5 One Leaves	G_1	P_{1leave}					
	.	P_{1stay}					
	.	.					
	G_n	$P_{n\text{-}stay}$					

* G represents experimental group. P represents individuals within each group. Groups 4 and 5 have individuals who leave and stay (P_{1stay}, P_{1leave}). In groups 4 and 5, leaving members represent one analytical condition, while staying members represent another.

Conditions. Main and interaction effect differences between the Control and other Analytical Conditions would indicate that the separation information had an effect. In other words, this analysis investigated whether the experiences of the Control group changed as a result of time and neutral information. Second, this analysis examined whether the experiences of other groups, such as the All Leave group, changed more than those of the Control group. This analysis used the same repeated measures analysis of variance model discussed above to examine each Analytical Condition versus the Control Condition.

A fifth analysis was performed to examine which differences across Periods within Analytical Conditions were significant. Each Analytical Condition was explored separately. For example, this analysis would show if the experiences of All Leave members changed as a result of reading the current event document. To do this, multiple analysis of variance (MANOVA) contrast tests were made of Period 3 with Periods 4 and 5 for each Analytical Condition. Again, the same repeated measures analysis of variance model discussed above was employed. A significant difference between Periods 3 and 4 would indicate that the individuals in the specific Analytical Condition were affected by the separation information. A significant difference between Periods 3 and 5 would indicate that the individuals in the specific Analytical Condition were affected by some combination of the separation information and the resultant group process.

The fourth quantitative analysis employed an analysis of variance of the group process questions (after-only) given in the fifth questionnaire. This represents the after-only portion of the design. This analysis is based on the model:

$$\text{item} = \text{intercept} + \text{Analytical Condition} + \text{error.}[2]$$

A significant main effect of this analysis would show differences in reported group process. In other words, a significant main effect would show that behavior occurring within the groups was different depending on the situation of the group. The analytic design also included an examination of the differences between simulation runs. This check was performed to identify differences between the responses from Michigan State and the two runs of Yale participants. This was accomplished by including a term for the simulation run and all relevant interaction terms in the above models. The precise aim of this analysis was to examine the strength of the simulation replications and to explore any unanticipated effects that could be revealed by the different settings. Only the One and Two Leave groups were included in this analysis because they were the only groups repeated across all three runs.

In addition to questionnaire data, observations during the simulation and subsequent debriefing sessions, and homework assignments and term papers were used to further explore the effects of the simulation and of separation anxiety in general. The qualitative data were analyzed to uncover patterns which emerged in reported group process, individual attitudes and emotions, and the relationship between the experience of separation anxiety as stimulated during the simulation to that experienced in other settings.

SUMMARY

The mergers and acquisitions simulation was designed to explore how employees in work groups respond emotionally and behaviorally to the fear and anxiety of separation caused by the announcement of a merger. Specifically, it was constructed to examine the impact of different numbers of staying and leaving members on individual and group emotions and behavior.

Five group conditions were included in the design: (1) Control group in which no separation information was given; (2) Others Leave group which was told that all group members will stay while others in their organization were to leave; (3) All Leave group where all members were to leave; (4) Two Leave group where two specific members were to leave; and (5) One Leaves group where one specific person was to leave. There were 119 participants (23 groups). The simulation was run three times yielding two replications.

The simulation began by assigning participants to groups. After an attachment building exercise the groups were informed that they were part of an organization that was undergoing a merger. They were also told that a specific individual(s) would be leaving their group. They then worked on a merger-related task.

Questionnaire instruments were constructed to gain repeated and after-only measures of individual emotional state, attitudes towards the group, and group process. A transitions distress questionnaire was also employed to gauge the effects of perceived transitions distress on individual responses. It was noted that the repeated measures questionnaire responses would be analyzed using a repeated measures design and the after-only measures would be analyzed using an after-only design. The transitions distress questionnaire items were to be included in quantitative analyses as a variable to check on the effects of prior separation experiences. Finally, qualitative data were collected in the form of observations during the simulation and debriefing sessions and each participant's term paper. These data were to be used to illuminate and enrich the quantitative results.

NOTES

1. In order to have the model correctly specified for the design set forth above, the actual model used for computing F-ratios, significance levels, and comparisons included a variable representing the simulation run and all its derivative interactions as terms:

scale = intercept + Run + Period + Analytical Condition +
Period*Analytical Condition + Run*Period + Run*Analytical
Condition + Run*Period*Analytical Condition + error

This model takes into account the effects of the different settings in which each simulation run took place.

2. In order to have the model correctly specified for the design set forth above, the actual model used for computing F-ratios, significance levels, and comparisons included a variable representing the simulation run and all its derivative interactions as terms:

item = intercept + Run + Analytical Condition +
Run*Analytical Condition + error

This model takes into account the effects of the different settings in which each simulation run took place.

4

Behavior During the Simulation: Quantitative Results

There are three questions which quantitative and statistical results are pivotal in helping to answer: What were the experiences of people who participated in the simulation? Are their experiences consistent with those predicted from the theory? Is it reasonable to assume that their experiences are not unique? The purpose of this chapter is to present the statistical results and the methods used to synthesize the raw questionnaire responses.

The analysis of the simulation data begins with an examination of the questionnaire instruments and scale creation. Fashioning scales from the questionnaires enables a concise reporting of experiences. Next, the results of an analysis of differences between the three runs of the simulation, including an analysis of the effects of perceived transitions distress, are presented. These data indicate the stability of the simulation results and help to answer the question of whether these results could be expected of anyone participating in the simulation.

The repeated measures data are reported next. These were collected five times over the course of the simulation. They exhibit how experiences changed as a result of the different exercises during the simulation. They also illustrate differences in reactions between the various analytical conditions. In other words, the repeated measures data answer the question: Do different numbers of people leaving influence how people feel and behave? Along with the repeated measures data, responses are graphically presented. These portray changes over the course of the simulation and illuminate statistical results.

Finally, the data collected after the simulation (after-only data) are reported. These data provide clear information about how people interacted in the various groups. They are also capable of depicting the effects of different numbers of people leaving on behavior.   Chapter 5 presents qualitative data that facilitate an empathic understanding of the statistical reports of the current chapter.   Chapter 6 connects both the statistical and qualitative results with theory.

SCALE CREATION

To simplify the statistical examination three scales were created. The scales represented (1) the transitions distress questionnaire, (2) the group attitudes section of the repeated measures questionnaire, and (3) the current emotions section of the repeated measures questionnaire.

Transitions Distress Scale

An oblique principal-components cluster analysis of the transitions distress questionnaire items yielded two primary clusters which explained 43 percent of the total variation. The first cluster explained 37 percent of the cluster variation (second eigenvalue = 1.72) and represented less stressful transitions. The second cluster explained 56 percent of the cluster variation (second eigenvalue = 0.95) and represented the more stressful transitions. The theme of Cluster 1 is moving, and people joining and leaving, while the theme of Cluster 2 is death and divorce. Cluster 2 was used as the Transitions Distress Scale in subsequent analyses because it represented the more stressful transitions and was therefore expected to be a better correlate of separation anxiety than the less stressful transitions of Cluster 1. Furthermore, on average, item-cluster correlations were higher in Cluster 2 (R^2 = 0.57) than they were in Cluster 1 (R^2 = 0.35). The six items which compose the Transitions Distress Scale are: sibling left home; parental divorce/separation; death of parent; death of sibling; death of child; and divorce/separation.

To determine the relationship of age to transitions distress participant age was correlated with the Transitions Distress Scale.   The Transitions Distress Scale correlated with participant age at a nonsignificant correlation of 0.09.

Group Characteristics and Emotion Scales

An oblique principal-components cluster analysis of the repeated measures·questionnaire items yielded two primary clusters which explained from 35 to 52 percent of the total variation in Periods 1, 3, 4, and 5.[1] One cluster represented the group attitudes items in the questionnaire and explained between 37 and 52 percent of the cluster variation (second eigenvalue range

= 1.28 to 2.07) in Periods 1 through 5. The scale created from this cluster was labeled Group Characteristics Scale. The ten items included in this scale are: I have made a large contribution to my group's work; The group enhances my ability to work; The group detracts from my ability to work; I am understood by my group's members; I understand my group's members; My group's members are open to my suggestions; I am open to the suggestions of my group's members; I like my group a great deal; I have a great sense of "feeling included" in my group; and I feel left out of my group. One item from the group attitudes section of the questionnaire—"The quality of my group's work is the best compared to all others"—was not included in the scale because it had a markedly lower correlation with the cluster (average R^2 with cluster in Periods 1 through 5 = 0.26) than all other items in the cluster (average R^2 with cluster in Periods 1 through 5 = 0.52). This item was analyzed separately in subsequent analyses.

The other cluster represented the current emotions section of the repeated measures questionnaire and explained between 33 and 52 percent of the cluster variation (second eigenvalue range = 2.07 to 2.27) in Periods 1 through 5. The scale created from this cluster was labeled Emotion Scale. The 20 items included in the Emotion Scale are Afraid, Angry, Anxious, Calm, Carefree, Comfortable, Confident, Content, Depressed, Happy, Jittery, Lonely, Nervous, On Edge, Pleased, Sad, Safe, Secure, Sure of Self, and Tense. Astrachan (1989) more fully describes the creation of the above scales.

DIFFERENCES BETWEEN RUNS

It was noted in Chapter 3 that the simulation was run three different times (1987, 1988, 1988) in two different settings (Yale University, Michigan State University) with two different sets of participants (Undergraduates and Masters students). In an effort to assess the independent influences of the three runs comparisons were made. Table 2 illustrates the differences in the Transitions Distress Scale and age of the participants. In general, the Yale University students were younger and reported higher transitions distress than the Michigan State University students.

Run comparisons were also made of participant experiences using a repeated measures analysis of variance[2] (repeated measures ANOVA). The One Leaves and Two Leave groups were included in the comparisons because they were the only ones simulated in each of the three runs. The results of these comparisons are given in Table 3. Run was a significant factor as part of an interaction in all three cases. This indicates that something associated with each run affected how people experienced the simulation. A further comparison was done to include the Transitions Distress Scale as a variable. The results of these analyses are presented in Table 4. Even with the inclusion of the Transitions Distress Scale as a variable, in two of the three

Table 2
Transitions Distress Scale Means and Participant Age by Run*

Run	Transitions Distress Scale Mean	Mean Participant Age
Yale University 1987	3.6	20.5
Michigan State 1987	3.3	26.6
Yale University 1988	3.6	21.8
Average	3.5	22.6

* Yale University 1987 and Michigan State University 1987 Transitions Distress Scale means were significantly different (Tukey's Studentized Range Test (HSD), alpha = 0.10).

cases above the Run term was significant as part of an interaction. However, the inclusion of the Transitions Distress Scale as a variable did result in fewer significant interactions that included the Run term and no significant effects which included the Run term in the Group Characteristics Scale.

REPEATED MEASURES DATA

Table 5 shows that of the 31 questionnaire items given in each of the five periods, every item and scale (100 percent) was significant either as a main effect for Period or Analytical Condition or as an interaction effect for Period by Analytical Condition using a repeated measures analysis of variance. This indicates that the simulation had an effect. Twenty-eight (90 percent) had a significant main effect for Period. This indicates that on average, all the groups changed over time. Twenty-five (81 percent) had significant Period by Analytical Condition interaction effects. This indicates that the Analytical Conditions changed differently over time.

In order to examine differences between periods MANOVA contrast tests for the Emotion Scale, Group Characteristics Scale, and the items Like Group, Feel Left Out, Feel Sad, and Feel Tense are presented in Table 6. In all seven cases, MANOVA contrast tests yielded significant ($p<0.05$) interaction effect differences between Periods 3 and 5. This indicates that Analytical Conditions changed differently from Period 3 (after group attachment formation and premanipulation) to Period 5 (end of simulation). In five of the seven cases MANOVA contrast tests showed significant ($p<0.05$) interaction effect differences between Periods 4 (after manipulation and before group interaction) and 5 (end of simulation).

To assess the effects of separation anxiety on the various Analytical Conditions, the Period effects experienced by the Control group and a

Table 3
Run Comparisons

ANOVA - Repeated Measures Significance Level								
Source	**Emotion Scale**			**Group Characteristics Scale**			**Work Quality Item**		
Condition								
(C)	ns			ns			ns		
Run (R)	**			ns			ns		
C * R	*			ns			ns		
Period (P)	***			***			**		
P * C	***			ns			*		
P * R	*			**			ns		
P * C * R	***			*			*		
Means for Period by Run								
Period	**3**	**4**	**5**	**3**	**4**	**5**	**3**	**4**	**5**
Yale 1987	3.95	3.35	3.72	4.28	4.12	3.97	3.29	3.52	4.33
Michigan 1988	4.27	3.95	4.13	4.06	3.98	4.13	3.79	3.69	3.59
Yale 1988	3.83	3.28	3.58	3.80	3.97	3.99	3.84	3.80	3.72

* = $p<0.05$; ** = $p<0.01$; *** = $p<0.005$; ns = not significant

comparison of the Period effects experienced by the Control group versus all other Analytical Conditions were explored. Table 7 displays the results of these analyses. This analysis shows how each analytical condition was similar to or different from the Control group.

The analysis of the Control group showed that there were significant main Period effects for both the Group Characteristics Scale and the Work Quality item. This indicates that, at least for this scale and item, the Control group participants changed over time. There was no main Period effect for the Emotion Scale, indicating that the emotions of the Control group members did not change over time.

The comparison of the Control group with the other Analytical Conditions indicates that all six comparisons had significant main Period effects for the Emotion Scale. Five had significant main Period effects for the Group Characteristics Scale and four had main Period effects for the Work Quality item. The significant Period effects indicate that on average all Analytical Conditions changed over the course of the simulation.

There were main Analytical Condition and interaction effects which included Analytical Condition for the Group Characteristics Scale in three of

Table 4
Run Comparisons with Transitions Distress Scale as a Variable

ANOVA - Repeated Measures Significance Levels			
Source	Emotion Scale	Group Characteristics Scale	Work Quality Item
Condition (C)	ns	ns	ns
Run (R)	ns	ns	ns
C * R	ns	ns	ns
Transitions (T)	ns	ns	ns
T * C	ns	ns	ns
T * R	ns	ns	ns
T * R * C	ns	ns	ns
Period (P)	ns	ns	ns
P * C	ns	ns	ns
P * R	ns	ns	ns
P * C * R	**	ns	ns
P * T	ns	*	ns
P * T * C	ns	ns	ns
P * T * R	ns	ns	ns
P * T * C * R	*	ns	*

* = $p < 0.05$; ** = $p < 0.01$; ns = not significant

the six comparisons. There were main Analytical Condition and interaction effects which included Analytical Condition for the Emotion Scale in five of the six comparisons, and there were main Analytical Condition and interaction effects which included Analytical Condition for the Work Quality item in five of the six comparisons. This suggests that for most of the comparisons, members of the Control group reported different experiences than participants in the other Analytical Conditions. Generally, the Control group members reported less positive emotion and lower work group quality than did members of the Others Leave and All Leave groups. Likewise, Control group members generally reported greater positive emotion and higher work group quality than did members of the One Leaves and Two Leave groups.

To help understand these results and the other repeated measures results mentioned above, charts were plotted of Analytical Condition means over three periods of the simulation (Figures 4-10). They display results for the scales and items depicted in Table 6. Each line represents one Analytical Condition. The charts show period plotted along the horizontal axis. The vertical axis is arranged such that the top represents more favorable responses, while the bottom corresponds to less favorable responses. The chart means were standardized to Period 3 for analytic purposes; each point represents the difference of the Analytical Condition mean with the corresponding mean at

Table 5
Significance Levels of Repeated Measures

Items	Period (P)	Condition (C)	Run	P*C
Work Quality	***	***	ns	**
Like Group	***	***	ns	***
Contribution to Group	ns	*	ns	*
Group Enhances Ability to Work	ns	*	ns	ns
Group Detracts from Ability to Work	*	ns	ns	***
Feel Included in Group	***	***	**	***
Understood by Group	***	ns	ns	ns
Understand Group Members	***	ns	ns	*
Group Members are Open to My Suggestions	***	ns	ns	ns
Open to Group Suggestions	**	ns	*	ns
Feel Left Out of Group	ns	ns	ns	**
Feel Afraid	***	ns	***	*
Feel Content	***	*	**	***
Feel Safe	***	ns	*	ns
Feel Depressed	***	ns	ns	**
Feel Secure	***	*	*	*
Feel on Edge	***	ns	**	*
Feel Angry	***	ns	ns	*
Feel Anxious	***	ns	ns	ns
Feel Lonely	*	ns	ns	*
Feel Happy	***	*	ns	***
Feel Sad	***	ns	ns	***
Feel Pleased	***	*	ns	***
Feel Sure of Self	*	ns	ns	***
Feel Carefree	***	ns	*	*
Feel Calm	***	ns	ns	***
Feel Tense	***	ns	ns	***
Feel Comfortable	***	ns	ns	***
Feel Confident	***	ns	ns	***
Feel Jittery	***	ns	ns	***
Feel Nervous	***	ns	ns	*
Scales				
Emotion	***	ns	ns	***
Group Characteristics	***	ns	ns	**

* = $p<0.05$; ** = $p<0.01$; *** = $p<0.005$; ns = not significant

Period 3. Period 3 was used as a baseline because it represents the time between attachment formation (i.e., after the group formation) and primary manipulation (i.e., when participants learned who was to leave). Differences

Table 6
MANOVA Contrast Test Significance Levels of Period (P) and Period by Condition Interaction Effects (P * C)

| Items | Contrast Periods | | | | | |
| | 3 & 4 | | 3 & 5 | | 4 & 5 | |
	P	P*C	P	P*C	P	P*C
Work Quality	ns	**	ns	*	ns	ns
Like Group	ns	ns	***	***	***	***
Feel Left Out	ns	ns	ns	***	ns	ns
Feel Sad	***	**	ns	**	***	*
Feel Tense	***	ns	ns	*	***	**
Scales						
Emotion	***	*	***	***	***	***
Group Characteristics	ns	ns	ns	***	ns	*

* = $p<0.05$; ** = $p<0.01$; *** = $p<0.005$; ns = not significant

between Period 3 and Period 4 represent the effects of the simulation manipulation by itself. Differences between Period 3 and Period 5 represent the effects of the simulation manipulation and the subsequent group process. This study primarily concerned how Period 3 (preseparation manipulation) differed with Periods 4 and 5 (postseparation manipulation).

In all seven charts, the Control group showed little change over Periods 3 through 5. With the exception of the Like Group item, the All Leave participants tended to be very positive about their group at the end of the simulation. Others Leave participants tended to be emotionally positive and in about the middle of all groups concerning their own group at the end of the simulation. Staying and leaving members of the Two Leave groups displayed divergent responses at Period 4 and convergent at Period 5. Frequently, the leaving members were negatively affected at Period 4 and then rebounded at Period 5. Staying and leaving members of the One Leaves groups were increasingly divergent in their responses from Periods 3 through 5. Leaving participants generally reported few dramatic effects at Period 4, and extreme adverse effects at the end of the simulation.

In order to examine which Analytical Conditions actually changed over time, MANOVA contrast tests were made of Period 3 with Periods 4 and 5 for each Analytical Condition. Table 8 shows the results of this analysis. Between Periods 3 and 4 (before and after the groups learned who would be leaving) only the Control group showed any significant differences in the Work Quality

Table 7
Significances of Control and Control Compared to Other Conditions

Analytical Condition Scale/Item	Period (P)	Condition (C)	Run (R)	P*C	P*R	C*R	P*C*R
Control (n=16)							
Group Characteristics Scale (GCS)	***	na	na	na	na	na	na
Emotion Scale	ns	na	na	na	na	na	na
Work Quality Item	**	na	na	na	na	na	na
Comparison of Control with: All Leave (n=15)							
GCS	ns	ns	ns	ns	ns	na	na
Emotion Scale	***	ns	ns	ns	***	na	na
Work Quality Item	ns	*	ns	*	*	na	na
Others Leave (n=11)							
GCS	***	ns	ns	ns	ns	na	na
Emotion Scale	***	ns	ns	*	***	na	na
Work Quality Item	***	ns	*	*	ns	na	na
One Leaves Leaving Members (n=9)							
GCS	***	ns	ns	***	ns	ns	***
Emotion Scale	***	ns	ns	***	***	ns	***
Work Quality Item	ns	**	ns	**	ns	ns	*
One Leaves Staying Members (n=36)							
GCS	***	ns	ns	ns	ns	ns	ns
Emotion Scale	***	ns	**	***	***	**	***
Work Quality Item	***	*	ns	*	**	ns	ns
Two Leave Leaving Members (n=12)							
GCS	***	ns	ns	**	*	*	ns
Emotion Scale	***	ns	ns	ns	**	ns	***
Work Quality Item	***	ns	ns	ns	ns	*	ns
Two Leave Staying Members (n=20)							
GCS	***	ns	ns	ns	ns	*	ns
Emotion Scale	***	ns	ns	**	***	ns	***
Work Quality Item	***	ns	ns	ns	ns	ns	ns

* = p<0.05; ** = p<0.01; *** = p<0.001; na = term does not exist; ns = not significant

item. They reported greater work quality. Only the Control group members reported significant differences between Periods 3 and 5 (after other groups

Figure 4
Emotion Scale Chart

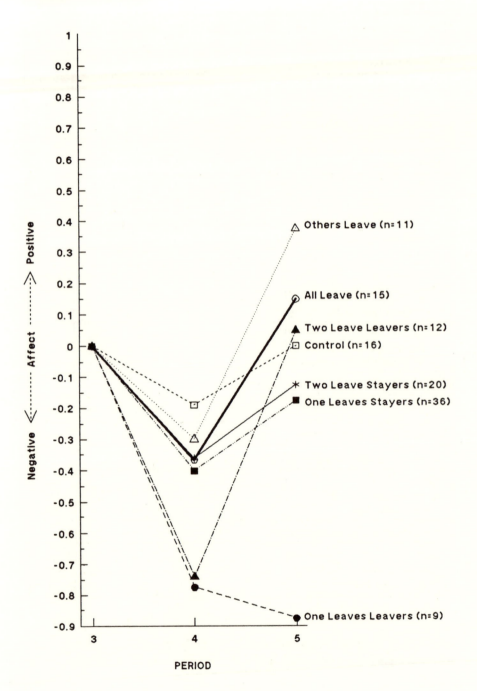

Figure 5
Group Characteristics Scale Chart

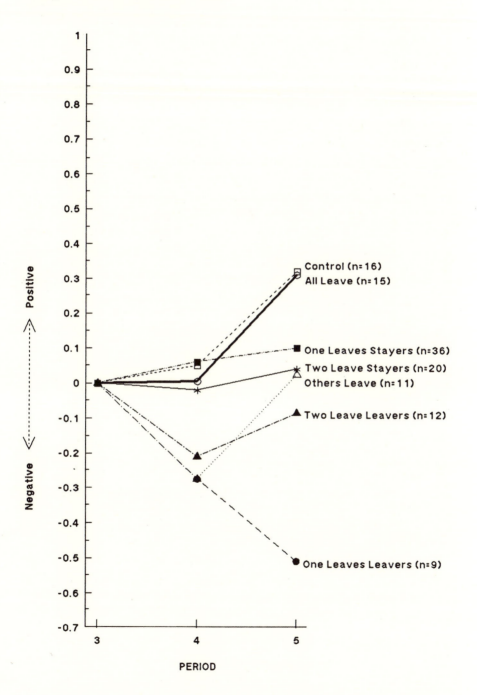

Figure 6
Work Quality Item Chart

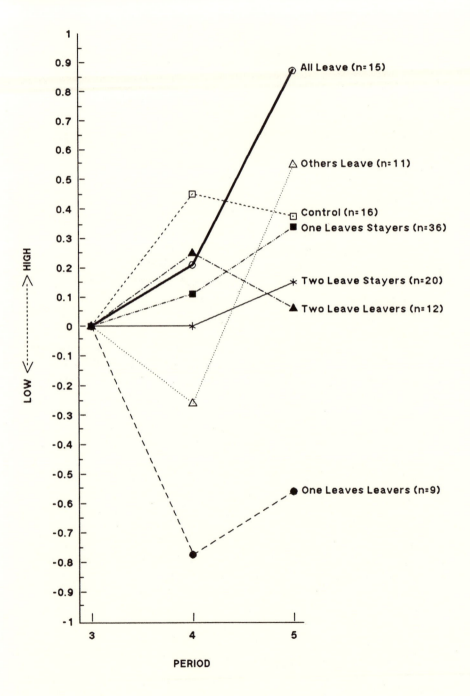

Figure 7
Like Group Item Chart

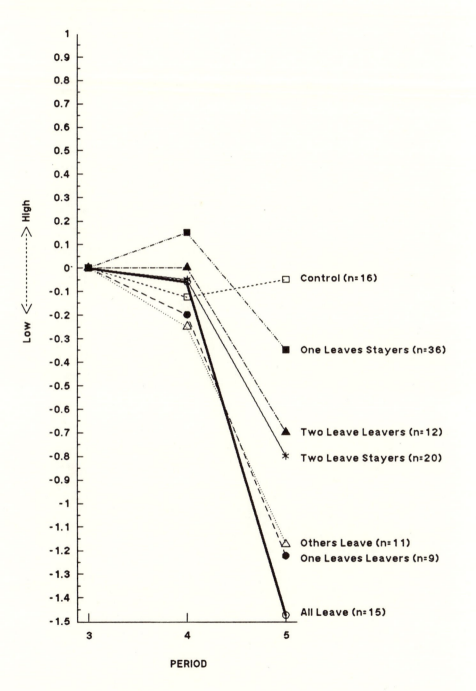

Figure 8
Feel Left Out Item Chart

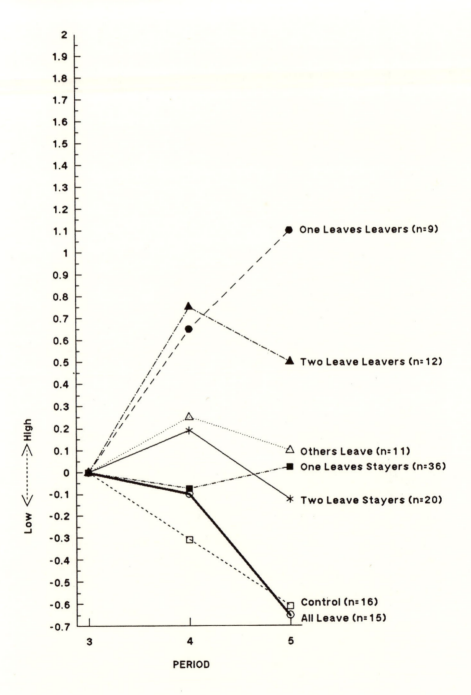

Figure 9
Feel Sad Item Chart

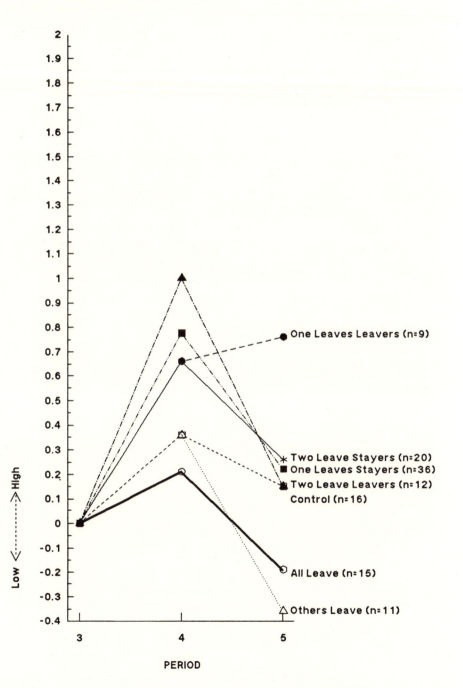

Figure 10
Feel Tense Item Chart

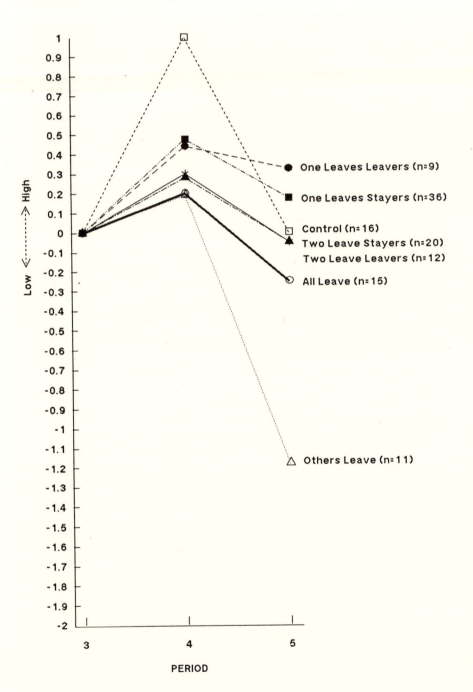

Table 8
Significances of MANOVA Contrasts of Within Condition
Between Period Differences (Period 3 with 4 and Period 3 with 5)

Analytical Condition Scale/Item	Period 3 with Period 4	Period 3 with Period 5
Control (n=16)		
Group Characteristics Scale	ns	**
Emotion Scale	ns	ns
Work Quality Item	**	ns
All Leave (n=15)		
Group Characteristics Scale	ns	ns
Emotion Scale	ns	ns
Work Quality Item	ns	ns
Others Leave (n=11)		
Group Characteristics Scale	*	ns
Emotion Scale	*	*
Work Quality Item	ns	*
One Leaves Leaving Members (n=9)		
Group Characteristics Scale	ns	ns
Emotion Scale	*	*
Work Quality Item	ns	ns
One Leaves Staying Members (n=36)		
Group Characteristics Scale	***	ns
Emotion Scale	ns	ns
Work Quality Item	ns	**
Two Leave Leaving Members (n=12)		
Group Characteristics Scale	ns	ns
Emotion Scale	**	ns
Work Quality Item	ns	ns
Two Leave Staying Members (n=20)		
Group Characteristics Scale	ns	ns
Emotion Scale	**	ns
Work Quality Item	ns	ns

* = p<0.05; ** = p<0.01; *** = p<0.001; ns = not significant

learned who was leaving and the end of the simulation) in the Group Characteristics Scale. Again, they reported a positive increase in their view of group characteristics. The Others Leave and the One Leaves groups' staying members displayed significant differences in the Group Characteristics Scale between Periods 3 and 4. The Others Leave, and One Leaves groups' leaving members, and both the staying and leaving members of the Two Leave groups reported significant differences in the Emotion Scale between Periods 3 and 4. The One Leaves groups' leaving members reported a negative change in emotion while the others reported a positive change in emotion between Periods 3 and 4. The Others Leave and the One Leaves groups' leaving members showed significant differences in the Emotion Scale between Periods 3 and 5. Again, the One Leaves groups' leaving members reported a negative emotional change while the Others Leave group members reported a positive emotional change between Periods 3 and 5. Finally, the Others Leave and the One Leave groups' staying members reported significant increases in the Work Quality item between Periods 3 and 5.

AFTER-ONLY MEASURES DATA

Table 9 shows that nine of the seventeen group process items (53%) had either a significant (p<0.05) main effect for Analytical Condition or an interaction effect which included Analytical Condition. Results of a comparison of means using Tukey's Studentized Range Test (HSD) are reported in Table 10.[3] Eleven of the seventeen items (65%) had significant differences in Analytical Condition means.

In general, the mean comparisons indicated that there were differences between the experiences of individuals across the seven Analytical Conditions. Generally, Control group members reported being the least affected by the simulation while leaving members reported being the most affected. Important specific observations from Table 10 are as follows: The Control group members were the most positive about their company's superiors while leaving members of the other groups were the most negative. The Two Leave groups' leaving members reported participating more than all other group members while the Two Leave groups' staying members reported participating less. The One Leaves groups' leaving members reported being the least close to their group after the simulation while the Two Leave groups' leaving members reported being the closest. Both the Control group members and the One Leaves groups' staying members reported that without them their groups' choice of which questions to ask the companies' CEOs would have been different. All Leave group members were lowest in reporting that the underlying issue that their group was dealing with was group separation, while both the Two Leave groups' staying members and the One Leaves groups' leaving members indicated most strongly that this was an issue of importance to their groups. The One Leaves groups' staying members, the Two Leave groups' leaving members, and Control group members were highest in reporting that individual separation was an issue which their groups

Table 9
Significances of Post-Simulation Only Items

Items	Condition (C)	Run (R)	C*R
Happy with company superiors	***	*	**
Angry with group	ns	ns	ns
Group chose best questions	ns	ns	ns
One member of Group was leader	ns	ns	ns
Participated more than all others in group	**	ns	ns
Closer to group after simulation ended	ns	ns	*
Without me, group choice would have been different	*	**	ns
Underlying issue was group separation	***	ns	ns
Underlying issue was individual separation	**	ns	ns
I had not a single strong alliance	ns	ns	ns
Two members were unfairly trying to influence	ns	ns	ns
One question chosen to satisfy leaving member(s)	*	ns	ns
After question to satisfy leaving member(s) chosen, group concentrated on the more important work of the task	ns	*	ns
I teamed up with one group member	*	ns	ns
Majority of the group did not want to discuss issues concerning leaving group member(s)	ns	ns	ns
I wanted to discuss issues concerning leaving group members far more than the rest	***	ns	***

* = p<0.05; ** = p<0.01; *** = p<0.001; ns = not significant

were dealing with, while the All Leave group members reported being affected by this issue the least. Control group members reported that no strong alliances were formed in the group and that they did not team up with any other single group member. On the other hand, the Two Leave groups' staying members reported that a strong alliance did form and the leaving members reported teaming up with another group member. All leaving members from the One Leaves, Two Leave, and All Leave groups reported that one question was chosen to satisfy a leaving member(s) after which the group went on to other work. The members of the All Leave group reported that the majority of the group did not want to discuss issues concerning a

Table 10
Order of Means and Significant Differences: Post-Simulation Items*

Analytical Conditions	Control Leave	Others Leave	All Leave	One Leaves Leavers	One Leaves Stayers	Two Leave Leavers	Two Leave Stayers
Happy with company superiors	A	AB	C	C	B	BC	B
Participated more than all others in group	A	B	AB	AB	AB	A	B
Closer to group after simulation ended	AB	AB	AB	B	AB	A	AB
Without me, group choice would have been different	B	A	AB	AB	B	AB	AB
Underlying issue was group separation	AB	AB	B	B	AB	AB	AB
Underlying issue was individual separation	A	AB	B	B	A	A	A
No single strong alliance formed	A	AB	AB	AB	AB	AB	AB
One question chosen to satisfy leaving member(s)	B	AB	A	A	AB	A	A
I teamed up with one group member	B	AB	AB	AB	AB	A	A
Majority of group did not want to discuss issues concerning leaving group member(s)	AB	AB	A	A	AB	AB	AB
I wanted to discuss issues concerning leaving group member(s) far more than the rest	D	BC	ABC	ABC	BC	AB	AB

* A = most positive	AB = no significant difference between A and B
B = second most positive	ABC = no significant difference between A, B, and C
C = third most positive	BC = no significant difference between B and C
D = fourth most positive	CD = no significant difference between C and D

leaving member(s), while the Two Leave groups' staying members indicated that the majority of the group did want to discuss those issues. Finally, the One Leaves groups' leaving members indicated that they wanted to discuss issues concerning a leaving member(s) more than the rest of their group. Control group members, followed closely by the Two Leave groups' staying members, wanted to discuss this issue the least.

SUMMARY

The data show that there was an effect due to the simulation. The differences between Analytical Conditions displayed in the data indicate that separation anxiety had an impact that was mediated by the number of people staying in and leaving the group. This was especially evident in emotional differences as shown by the repeated measures results for the Emotion Scale. Additional support for the differences between Analytical Conditions was given by the after-only results. It was further seen that these results were stable as they were consistent after two replications in two different settings. It was also seen that differences between settings could be partially explained by differences in reported transitions distress. The specific processes by which the differences between conditions arose are illuminated in the narrative reports discussed in Chapter 5. The link between the statistical results and theory is more fully developed in Chapter 6.

NOTES

1. Results from Period 2 were not included in the analysis because one of the groups did not return questionnaires for that period. This should have made the analysis more conservative because one of the repeated measures was not included.

2. Throughout this text, all repeated measures analysis of variance probabilities are adjusted by the Greenhouse-Geisser (1970) Method which tries to take into account the correlations inherent in a repeated measures design by altering the degrees of freedom. Further, all sums of squares were calculated using type IV sums of squares.

Unless otherwise stated, all tests for sphericity of orthogonal components, using Mauchly's criteria (Huynh & Feldt, 1970) or MANOVA tests using the Hotelling-Lawley Trace Statistic (Freund et al., 1986) indicated that the assumption of statistical independence of repeated measures was supported.

3. Mean comparisons using Tukey's Studentized Range Test (HSD) are not as sensitive to differences as the repeated measures analysis of variance. However, repeated measures were not feasible for the group process items because the content of the questions had the potential to interfere with group process.

5

Qualitative Results from the Simulation

Quotations provided by students' term papers offer a rich source for understanding what was experienced during the simulation. The majority of this chapter recounts participant experiences in their own words to add substance to the quantitative results. The chapter proceeds with a brief statement about how prevalent discussions of separation anxiety and the simulation were in the term papers. Next, the difficulty people experienced in engaging the issue of separation anxiety is mentioned. It continues with the actual experiences of members in each condition and concludes with a short description of what was observed during the simulation and debriefing sessions.

TERM PAPERS

Though only 3 of 26 class sessions (11 percent including the simulation class) were devoted to separation anxiety, it was discussed in 99 percent of the papers and was explored with some depth[1] in 86 percent of the papers. The simulation was addressed in 42 percent of the papers and examined in depth[2] in 31 percent of the papers. Table 11 displays the number of participants in each Analytical Condition by the degree to which separation anxiety was discussed. Table 12 displays the number of participants in each Analytical Condition by the degree to which the simulation was examined.

Table 11
Degree to Which Separation Anxiety Was Discussed by Condition*

Condition (% of condition)	Discussed In-depth	Mentioned	Not Addressed
Control	12 (100%)	0 (0%)	0 (0%)
All Leave	15 (100%)	0 (0%)	0 (0%)
Others Leave	10 (91%)	1 (9%)	0 (0%)
One Leaves Leaving Members	5 (100%)	0 (0%)	0 (0%)
One Leaves Staying Members	19 (95%)	1 (5%)	0 (0%)
Two Leave Leaving Members	6 (75%)	1 (13%)	1 (13%)
Two Leave Staying Members	11 (79%)	3 (21%)	0 (0%)
TOTAL	**78 (92%)**	**6 (7%)**	**1 (1%)**

* Michigan State University participants were not included because they did not prepare final papers. Further, chi-square tests were not significant.

Table 12
Degree to Which the Simulation Was Discussed by Condition*

Condition (% of condition)	Discussed In-depth	Mentioned	Not Addressed
Control	4 (33%)	1 (8%)	7 (58%)
All Leave	6 (40%)	1 (7%)	8 (53%)
Others Leave	4 (33%)	2 (18%)	5 (45%)
One Leaves Leaving Members	3 (60%)	0 (0%)	2 (40%)
One Leaves Staying Members	5 (25%)	1 (5%)	14 (70%)
Two Leave Leaving Members	1 (16%)	2 (25%)	5 (63%)
Two Leave Staying Members	3 (21%)	3 (21%)	8 (57%)
TOTAL	**26 (31%)**	**10 (12%)**	**49 (58%)**

* Michigan State University participants were not included because they did not prepare final papers. Further, chi-square tests were not significant.

Engaging Separation Anxiety

While a high percentage of papers dealt with separation anxiety in depth, several did not. It may be that they found it too uncomfortable to begin thinking about separation anxiety. Indeed, many students reported great difficulty in beginning their exploration of separation anxiety. One student, whose paper focused on separation anxiety, provided a list of all the things used as diversions so that she could avoid thinking about the issues that she eventually wrote about:

Avoidance behavior: Filed my nails, talked on the phone to my sister, reread back issues of every available newspaper and mail order catalogue, eaten two hour lunches, worked on a paper due next week, talked to my roommates, wrote letters, cleaned my room, doodled, played tennis (at least an hour a day every day I was writing), gossiped with everyone I knew in the library, daydreamed, picked out courses for next year, read a cookbook, made a tape of music to run to, picked out a mother's day card (it took me an hour), wrote a short story, experimented with shades of eyeshadow. I hope this list conveys a sense of how hard it was for me to write this paper. For every hour I spent at my keyboard, I must have spent three trying to avoid doing just that.

However difficult it may have been for the majority of students to get started, once they began addressing separation anxiety, their inhibitions seemed to give way to many examples and much exploration. This is also evident in one members' recollections of the simulation debriefing:

During the debrief on separation, many people started by saying that separation really did not affect them, and then after a few minutes of talking, they told the class how separation has affected them, and was still affecting them in their everyday interactions. A lot of people had suppressed, and not come in touch with the feelings that occurred during separation. This discussion helped me to open some doors of experiences in the past which I may have shut too soon because of the pain involved.

Experiences of One Leaves Groups' Leaving Members

Those chosen to leave in the One Leaves groups articulated a consistent view which included heightened anxiety, withdrawal, and an overall depressed emotional state. One individual discussed his feelings of isolation and compared them to his athletic team experiences:

Before I received my pink slip, I was very active in group discussions and felt like I was an important part of the corporation. All of my emotions toward the group, however, changed once I discovered I was fired. I no longer considered myself a group member. A pink slip from another group [Two Leave group] tried to fight his being dismissed. However, I took the route of almost feeling sorry for myself because I felt lost from my group. I felt helpless and lost. Everything that was discussed after that in the group, I took no part in. I even felt that our group did a poor job after my dismissal because the group was no longer receiving any of my inputs. There were also feelings of guilt in my mind because I realized that the other group members were making compromises for me. They wanted to ask questions that pertained to me and my future. I couldn't understand why they were worrying about me because I already considered my position finalized. I know that this was just an exercise, however, I even noticed changes in the other members' emotions after I received the pink slip. Their anxiety levels seemed to go up when they realized that

I had been fired. It may have been because they felt sorry for me. However, I don't think that was the case. I believe they felt more anxious and showed signs of sorrow because they were so relieved to have not been the one who had been fired. I can clearly see how this could relate to real life instances.

The thing that hit home the most from the exercise was how group behavior changes when there is a separation within a group. Everything can be going along smoothly when suddenly one member's position is changed and it affects the whole group. I remember one instance where one of our teammates broke his leg. . . . [W]e'd been on a winning streak up until this guy got hurt. I remember thinking at the time that we wouldn't be all that affected by this kid's absence, since he wasn't one or our better players. However, with this kid gone, we couldn't win games. There was just a feeling of something missing on the field and in the locker room.

Another (pseudonym Sarah) went into more detail in discussing her feelings of withdrawal and isolation. Initially, she saw her feelings and behavior changing as a result of the merger news:

As soon as all the papers were handed out, I noticed that all the other members in my group had yellow sheets. I knew immediately that this meant that I was different and the pink color of my paper had to have some designated meaning. Therefore I jokingly asked A if she wanted to change sheets. I was anxious to find out what my pink sheet meant. . . . Before I knew what the pink sheet symbolized, I heard A respond, "Oh Sarah." Soon everybody in the group was staring at me with sympathetic eyes. I was so nervous I could not even concentrate on what I was reading. . . . From the reaction of my group members, I knew I had been labeled as something terrible. My ability to comprehend what I was reading decreased rapidly because I was too concerned about my label. Soon I saw the bold face letters, "you will be asked to leave", and it became clear why the members were behaving in a sympathetic manner.

Immediately I felt separated from my group. I was an outsider. I did not even participate in the task. . . . Since I was not going to be a member of the company I did not care what questions the other members of my group selected. I quickly skimmed over the questions as the other members carefully studied the choices. Unfortunately I did not notice that three of the questions concerned employees who were being asked to leave. My resistance to participate in this task caused me to overlook questions which were beneficial to my future.

When interaction began taking place, she began to view her feelings and behavior as being strongly influenced by the other members of her group. She also described many behaviors that indicated the formation of a boundary between her and the staying members of her group:

B suggested a question which she believed should be asked first. She explained the economic details which told why this question was important. I personally did not understand any part of B's explanation and had no intention of trying to comprehend her reasoning because I did not belong to the group. I just wanted the task to end.

Next, A proposed that we first ask a question which concerned me, the person who was leaving. At this point I realized that I was not completely excluded from the task. Some of the questions were relevant to me. However, B did not think they should waste a question on me because I was leaving anyway. She asked the group, "Are we going to cover *our* asses or the entire groups' asses." This use of the word "our" verified that there was a definite separation. The members of the group decided that the first question should address me, since the work group was supposed to be very close.

. . . After B expressed her desire to ignore the questions concerning the employee leaving, I became very critical of all her comments. For example, at one point during the discussion she asked if I had any suggestions for questions concerning the members who would remain working. She probably did this because I remained very quiet after the question dedicated to me was chosen. B was probably trying to include me in the task. However, I did not appreciate her attempt. Instead I found it very ironic that she wanted me to help choose a question to help the members remaining at work when she did not even want there to be a question asked about the people leaving work. Also, a comment that she made at the finish of the task really upset me. A couple of people said they were sorry that I got fired. I appreciate their concern. B expanded on this comment by replying, "I have a job for you at the Deli spreading mustard." I despised this statement. I found it very degrading.

This final incident illustrates how strong an emotional impact the simulation generated. Another student recounted how she actively withdrew herself from the group. She began interpreting the behavior of her group from the vantage point of an outsider:

I was the only person in my group who got a pink sheet. I claimed to be excited to have the different one, but the truth is that I was mortified to be singled out. . . . My group was extremely concerned with this fired person, me, and the entire conversation was around this subject. My reaction to the whole scenario was one of doubt. I felt like the people in my group over did it with the concern for me and forgot to think about themselves. I did not understand such behavior and immediately classified them as hypocritical.

She was then able to connect her experiences in the simulation with her family relationships and in the process reinvents a piece of the concepts of splitting and projection:

Then I began to investigate things from a different angle. First I placed where this obsession with fakeness and hypocrisy came from: my mother. I was attributing feelings and concerns and even identity doubts to other people instead of facing them in relation to myself. It is relevant that I would be questioning other people's motives just so I would not have to face mine. There is a certain guilt in me looking at my own motives when unconsciously I know that they are not the best ones.

In general, the leaving members of the One Leaves groups reported an anxious response to the merger news. During the discussion, they experienced their group members as behaving in ways that encouraged further withdrawal and detachment.

Experiences of One Leaves Groups' Staying Members

The reactions and observations of the staying members in the One Leaves groups further illuminates the interchange between staying and leaving members:

As I stated before, I have discovered that my initial reaction to such a situation [imminent separation] is to "professionalize" the matter. The assignment of mergers and acquisitions prepared the perfect field in which I could do just that. I am taking several courses dealing with M & A [Mergers and Acquisitions] case studies specifically. The consequences to business and society of such industrial change are now part of my carnal knowledge. Backed by this wisdom, I attempted to lead the group to realize the technicalities of the merger. My explanations on how the corporate decisions would impact the employee's job security, the stock plan, the options plan, the new company's need for quick capital to pay off debts acquired thus the dispensability of parts of the firm such as human relations), and the effect of possibly moving the headquarters away from the community seemed unimportant to the rest of my group, as they were more concerned about the welfare of their soon-to-be separated friend.

I had resigned myself to the fact that he would not be able to retain his position in the company, therefore, he should not have needed to play a role in our decision making process to determine which questions to ask the CEOs of the company. Others in the group picked up on the coldness of my attitude towards our friend. My uncaring nature when initially dealing with separation issues was all too apparent. Although they set me straight and convinced me that my behavior was entirely too corporate and inappropriate concerning someone I should care for, I would still only permit the group to "donate" him one question: "What efforts will be made to support the employee until such time at which his next job is secured."

During the ensuing debriefing experience, C revealed his pain from exclusion that he felt from the group simulation exercise. It was the exclusion which I had helped to foster. It would not absolve the crass behavior which I had displayed to apologize and admit my shame for my actions and words. I said I was sorry in any case. My recognition of my harsh, unemotional behavior solidified the problem in my mind that I seem to reject the feelings behind bonds formed as I am confronted with a separation issue and deal with loss in a very cold, stone-faced way.

Another student expressed how she attempted to try to help the leaving member feel better and a part of the group:

When it came time for my group to decide the three questions we wanted to ask our company, we each chose three questions by ourselves and compared choices. I thought that it was crucial for us to help D, who was fired, in any way that we could, by asking a question about his future, while everyone else thought that it was important to think about the remaining part of our group's future with our new company. As I have exhibited before, I was concerned with helping others. My first reaction, when I was reading my yellow sheets, was to laugh and say, "Oh, no!", when I got to the part that said D was being fired. Then I felt relieved that I was not being asked to leave, and I felt horrible for D. . . .

D first withdrew from the discussion, because he felt isolated from the rest of the group that was primarily concerned with themselves and not D, but then he started to give input to our discussions, as soon as I said that I thought that we should give special attention to helping him out. Simply by showing my support and care for him, D became involved with our group discussion. I often react the same way to situations, in that I withdraw and sulk when I do not feel that people care about me or my opinions, and then as soon as someone makes me feel included, I become a participating member of the group again. The issues relate to my feelings of isolation within my family. I really felt pleased with myself when D expressed in the debrief, how I was the only one who showed sincere interest in him in our group. It made me happy to know that I could make someone feel somewhat included in an isolated situation, that I would despise being in.

It was not clear from the debriefing sessions or term papers that the excluded person in the above group actually felt included.

One student recounted the complexity of personal feeling as a staying member in a One Leaves group. These included initial feelings of relief, followed by frustration and anger at her group and the company's superiors, some anxiety, and a sense of loss.

The mergers and acquisition simulation that we conducted in class also revealed the high level of separation anxiety and loss felt when separated from someone to whom you have not been attached very long. The simulation was even more powerful, because the attachments were created artificially; yet I felt a real sense of loss when we realized that E was to leave our group. I identified very strongly with the fact that she was not only essential to our work group, but to our social lives outside of work as well. The work group was supposed to be "second only to your family" in importance in my life. . . . Our group was unique and the more into the simulation we got, the more boundaries our group had which gave us a distinct identity as a group and distinguished us from other groups. By the time I read the company history and current event I was convinced that we were the best group and no one in our group should have been asked to leave. On the contrary, at the very beginning, before our group had established boundaries I was not as ready to agree that my group was going to be the best group. But after we were given a particular place to meet particular coworkers, a group number, had formed a psychological contract, and had read the company history, I felt we were a real group.

When I discovered that E was the one of us asked to leave, I felt relief at first, but it did not last very long. Soon relief became fear that they could ask any one of the rest of us in the group to leave, frustration with anger toward the executive officer of my company, sympathy for E, and loss from having her taken away from the group. In general, our group's first priority was to ask questions which dealt with the problem of E's dismissal. We considered asking questions which asked that she stay, but decided that according to the information given on the Current Event form —"the decision was final" and "it was highly unlikely that she would rejoin the company" —there was not much chance of preventing it. At this point I felt that E's dismissal was unjust and I noticed how she felt really separate from the group task even though we were trying to include her. She would say such things as "I think *you all* should pick that question" or "If I were *you*, I would choose this question." She kept on saying "you all" instead of "we." We also felt separate from her. The discussion revolved around what "we" were going to do for E. By this time I felt angry that our group was being broken up; our group boundaries were being torn down. I began to think that if we didn't have E, then we wouldn't be the same group anymore and we would not be able to perform the quality work for which our team was known. So I suggested that we all quit. The others did not chime in at first, but then I told them that we could all find positions in a company that was a little more loyal to its employees who have been so loyal to them. Also, there was not much of a chance of advancing in Streamline. Our final decision was to wait on any drastic decisions until we asked our questions of the executive officers.

The same individual recounted the following from the subsequent debriefing sessions. Here she discusses other group members' behavior and she explores the roots of her own feelings and behavior:

During the debriefing session of the staying members of the One Leaves group, there were mixed experiences. F said that he only picked questions which pertained to the leaving person to "appease her" and not to look like the bad guy. The rest of the people in my group felt relieved to discover that they were not the fired person as I did at first, also, but I did not feel secure. I still felt anxious about maybe being fired, while G and H felt that they weren't going to be fired now or in a month. I felt dispensable. I told my group that if they just randomly fired E, why should I feel any more secure in my job since we were on the same level and especially since, as a Black woman in the company I could be seen as especially by the new management as expendable. H asked me if I really thought about being a Black woman and being fired and I told her that I did. However, the primary reason I felt my job was not safe was because someone else in my exact same position was fired. On our debriefing sheet we wrote, "relief, anxiety for *self* and *one being fired.*"

In one paper, an individual made the direct comparison between her experience as a staying member of the One Leaves group to her earlier experience as a leaving member in an athletic group:

The whole idea of a group working together toward a common cause recalled in my memory a similar group experience in my life. When I was a sophomore in high school, three of us from the gymnastics club were groomed for a major international competition to be held in Rotterdam, Holland. It was a large team effort. . . . It is difficult to describe the bonding that went on. We even developed coded words and signals to relay encouragement and enthusiasm.

After several months of intense coaching with physical and psychological training, we went to Denver in order to put together the American team that would go to Rotterdam. I, along with my partner, did not make the team. Our friend did. Both of us who were cut were asked by the group to go to Rotterdam as spectators. I was able to go. . . . However, my partner lacked the resources to make the trip.

This put me in an extremely interesting situation. In one way, I was a staying member of the group, with the friend who stayed behind as the leaving member. However, in another way, I was a leaving member because we no longer really shared the same goal. Of course, I wanted my talented friend to do well, but I also felt very removed from the group task.

In the classroom simulation of the merger and acquisition exercise, I was told that I would be staying in my job. Only J was asked to leave our group of five members. I think my past experience with respect to the competition greatly influenced my behavior in the classroom experiment. First, it recalled feelings of somehow being different from other group members. Although I was still part of the group that went to Rotterdam, in my eyes, we were there for a very different purpose than I had anticipated. The attention was no longer on the three of us, but on the one of us.

I had some trouble dealing with this. I partially believed that I had failed and that my presence on the trip was some kind of token consolation prize. The others in the group did not treat me that way at all. On the contrary, they attempted to include me in on all the events, problems, and decision-making that went on. I remember in particular their asking me for input regarding non-gymnastics oriented activities. If there was interest, I would look into tours or special events to occupy us. I was sort of made the unofficial entertainment guide for the small amount of time that wasn't dedicated to practicing, performing, eating, relaxing, or sleeping.

I guess this generally made me feel good—being given some sort of responsibility and area of control. And yet, I seem to remember times when I would resent the same responsibility, feeling that it was simply a method to get me out of the way. . . . I was insecure about my own worth as well as the group's attachment and interest in me.

This experience affected the way I dealt with J's leaving the group. . . . I tried to make her feel as comfortable as possible with the group and with the task. The others in the group also seemed to want this. . . . At the outset, we brought up the topic of the employees who were asked to leave the company. We decided that this topic merited enough attention to devise our own question. As a result, we spent a lot of time on this issue, trying to create a question that forced our superiors to pursue options other than job termination. We were also concerned that some kind of support system be established to help those whose jobs must be eliminated.

While I wanted to make J comfortable with her place in the group, I simultaneously remember feeling that to over stress the issue of terminated employees would make her feel singled out. . . . Thinking about it after, I felt ashamed because I thought that my concern for her was really just a rationalization of selfish desires to get off the topic. . . . I think that my concern for J's feeling singled out by so much talking about job termination grew from my experiences in Rotterdam. . . . I transposed this experience onto the class simulation, where I anticipated that J would feel singled out in the discussion of job elimination and termination.

I think there is evidence that this assessment of the situation was correct. J, of course, participated in the discussions that related most specifically to her, as was expected, but she was also actively working against this. It was intriguing that she persistently proclaimed that we, the remaining group members, should watch out for ourselves. At least three times during the group session, she suggested that we ask about changes in the pay scale. . . . By changing the emphasis of the concern to address questions that were more to our benefit than hers, she was minimizing the attention on her as the "leaving member." . . . The contentment I felt with the unofficial job I was given was because I was freed from interacting only in the gymnastics environment in which I felt singled out. This established an ironic pattern: by being removed from the primary focus of the group (the competition), I felt more like a member of the group than if my only diversion had been that focus.

She then went on to discuss how she felt increasingly distanced from and angry with the gymnastics world and sought college as a diversion. After reflecting on these experiences, she wrote that she still had a yearning to be part of the gymnastics scene.

In general, the staying members of the One Leaves groups behaved in ways that served to exclude the leaving member. They also recognized that part of their behavior grew from their feelings of discomfort.

Experiences of Two Leave Groups' Staying Members

Common to both One Leaves and Two Leave groups was that staying members experienced relief when they learned that they were not going to be asked to leave. One staying member of a Two Leave group wrote:

The very first thing I wrote in my journal about my simulation group was, "This group sucks. We're talking about B.S." Later in the simulation, after we had received our instructions on who was being fired and who retained, I wrote: "Notice that two members of the group got canned—I'm not one of them—I like this, it's kind of fun."

Another member of a Two Leave group expressed his relief in the following passage:

I remember being so thankful and perceptibly happy that I was not one of the group members chosen to be "fired" (my group had two people leave). I think if I had been cut out, I would have gotten very upset, and felt singled out, and would have attributed some ulterior motive to the choice. I felt very safe and pleased that I was allowed to stay, probably because I have a hard time feeling left out because of my family dynamics and my previous experiences in groups.

Another student also indicated relief and acknowledged the quick formation of a boundary around the staying members, "As we read our task sheets we all giggled as we read the line that told us that the pink sheeted people were going to be let go. We laughed because we were not the ones that had to go. Our knowledge of their plight bonded us together."

Staying members of the Two Leave groups were confronted by leaving members who did not withdraw:

When we all realized that the two pink sheets were going to leave they were immediately set outside the rest of us who were staying. Where we were once one group cooperating and communicating, we were now suddenly split in two. The two groups now had distinctly different agendas for the questions that we were going to ask. With different fates facing the two groups, we were set up in an adversarial relationship against the pink sheets. We had to work hard to compromise and find a solution to our differences. I think that the fact that we had communicated and were bonded before the circumstances were changed made a big difference in the effectiveness of our discussion. Each side was firm in what it thought we should ask, each had their own ideas. We were able to compromise and give the people that were leaving a question. As I said in class, in a real live situation, behavior in the M & A exercise would hardly be as civil.

In my summer job at National Utility this past summer, I watched several of my friends and coworkers struggling to keep their jobs in the wake of tremendous job cutting. Each person was intent on covering their backside at the expense of others. In the environment filled with adversity some of them retreated and left with a negotiated settlement. This behavior was like what I saw in the group. One of the people that was fired was willing to simply accept his fate and move on. From my own life experience, I gained new insight into how easy a group can fall apart when security is stripped away from an environment. People in group discussions in class were concerned with themselves and not anyone else. Cooperation was not that good and proceeded to deteriorate as time passed. In the real life situation everyone became isolated and defensive, less friendly, and more aggressive. . . . I did not want to give the people being fired a question.

He continues to examine the theme of the power of circumstances as he recounts how the staying and leaving members rapidly began competing with one another:

In the M & A experiment, the people who were getting fired in our group worked together against those of us who were staying on. Instead of remaining a harmonious group, changing circumstances split us up. Before anyone was told they were going to be fired, we had all communicated and formed a small bond of cooperation within the group. When the rules of the game changed, the people that were fired were pitted against us and there was adversity and confrontation where there once was cooperation and discussion. The group was split in two by circumstances, not by radical personal changes.

A staying member discussed how his experiences as a Black man contributed to his anxiety:

The simulation on separation caused a lot of gut feelings for me. My group lost two people, a black woman and a white man. I immediately connected with the pink sheeted people. I thought that the black woman had got the axe legitimately but the white man had been informed by mistake. To me, this simulation was not on separation but on the anxiety blacks have around employment. The saying "last hired and first fired," is no myth. . . . What shocked me was the inability of people remaining in the group to realize that now they were on the bottom of the company and the next in line out the door. . . . I wanted to give all the questions to the people leaving because I identified with them the most. People in my group could not identify at all with the unemployed group.

Staying members of the Two Leave group reported that the merger news caused a barrier to grow in their groups. They also reported that staying and leaving members were "pitted against" one another leading to heightened conflict within the group.

Experiences of Two Leave Groups' Leaving Members

While leaving members initially experienced a sense of exclusion and isolation, they soon joined forces to become included in the group. One participant recounted his experience during the simulation as follows:

In the separation simulation all I wanted to do initially was find another job. It seems like when separation comes, all I want to do is find something else to become attached to. K, my partner, wanted to keep his job, and I felt basically out of it because it made no difference to me. If they did not want me, I did not want them. K kept insisting and we actually got two of the three questions to be on our behalf. Even though I was not participating a great deal, the fact that the questions seemed to favor us made me somehow feel more a part of the group and made me happy about the fact that they cared for me. K's insistence gave him control of the situation because he had something to fight for, whereas everyone else in the group did not. Their status basically remained the same, so they had nothing to really fight for and we did.

The leaving members of the Two Leave groups corroborated the events described by the staying members. They also indicated that they had a vested interest in staying in the group and felt supported in their efforts to do so.

Experiences of All Leave Group Members

Members of the All Leave group identified the close bonding that occurred as well as the denial and suppression of emotions and issues concerning separation.   One member of an All Leave group made an interesting comparison with the class group and a clique of friends.

[M]y All Leave group reminded me of my circle of senior friends. The All Leave group tended to deny separation. We chose the questions which would be the most beneficial to the company as a whole. . . . We did our job exactly as we would have done it had we all been staying. We gave no special emphasis to questions pertaining to leaving. Furthermore, some of our members (including me) maintained that there was a chance that we would not be laid off. Similarly, many of my senior friends continue to go about their business as if separation is not on the horizon. Some of these friends . . . continue to work as hard as ever, sacrificing many opportunities to participate in senior events. Several seniors I know also plan on spending their summer in the area, as if it will make separation from here more gradual and easier to deal with (in fact, I might be one of them).

Another individual discussed the high degree of bonding that occurred in his All Leave group:

After class I asked myself, what just went on there? I noticed that the five in our group formed our own sort of organization. We were then separated from a larger organization, which forced us to become closer among ourselves. I realized that this is what occurs in ordinary situations where group members must face separation. In other words, when a group of people are all involved in a separation, they seek security of some sort. In this instance we sought to "stick together" and organize ourselves. I feel that this correlates closely with the idea of separation in everyday life. For even in the instance of death, we seek to find comfort with those around us that have experienced the same sort of separation as we have. . . . I felt a loyalty to them, and a sense of companionship.   As M stated, "There was a sense of homogeneity within the group. No one had a leg up on the other, and therefore there was no need for any of us to take a contradictory stand toward the issues." Therefore, we were all content and worked together to decide upon the three questions which we wished to ask.

In general, members of the All Leave groups experienced a high level of bonding and portrayed a desire to avoid potentially painful topics.

Experiences of Others Leave Group Members

While members of the Others Leave groups felt some separation anxiety, they reported relatively little discomfort and little reason to deny the impact of the upcoming, simulated separation. One individual put it succinctly:

Both the nature of the exercise and the realization that the semester was winding down made me feel the pangs of separation. I did not feel the same degree of separation as other groups who were leaving or who had associates leaving, yet even if it was imagined, I felt an air of separation from the laid-off workers whom I had probably hired.

My group experienced no separation, felt little anxiety, and worked together very effectively. In fact, the quality of our work got better as the hour progressed. We already knew each other and the task intrigued us, so serious discussion and decision-making were viable at the outset.

Experiences of Control Group Members

The experience of Control Group members was characterized by security and high morale as reported in the following excerpt:

I was skeptical when my group decided that we would stick together, no matter what happened. Deep inside I expected that at some point I would either need to compromise and suppress my individuality or break the pact. Unfortunately, in my group nothing happened, i.e. the company continued unchanged, and so we did not have a chance to test our bonding. The subsequent debriefing session revealed that the groups such as ours for which there was no significant occurrence left the simulation with the sense that we did not gain much from the exercise as the other groups. Not having to worry firsthand about the emotional issues relating to separation, we became secure with our status in the company. The high morale fostered a real team spirit in the group that continued to the end of the simulation.

Another participant confirmed this report:

I was in the group that lost no one, so our initial response was, "what's the point?" As one group member put it, initially, "we just cruised through and thought it was a big joke." . . . What I did feel was a high group morale and team spirit. We were suspicious as to what was going to merge or be acquired, and we vowed to stay together even if they tried to break us up. We were all secure in our status within the company, and as N put it, we realized that, "life goes on when things are going good."

OBSERVATIONS

Observations during the simulation and the debriefing sessions confirmed the reports contained in the term papers. During the first debriefing session, leaving members of the One Leaves groups reported that they had been cut out of their groups, not at all invited to participate as contributing group members, not asked about feelings, and they generally reported feeling discriminated against and alone. One participant said that she gained a greater understanding of an earlier exercise on discrimination and intergroup dynamics. She said, "I now understand what Gary [pseudonym] was talking about after the Collared Exercise[3]—people who were not in my situation could not then and cannot now understand what I was going through." Observation of the staying members of the One Leaves groups during the simulation revealed an initial and momentary outpouring of sympathy. Staying members used such words as, "I feel sorry for you," and, "is there anything I can do [to make you feel better]." This initial reaction was followed by an almost complete lack of communication with leaving members. For example, there was little eye contact or verbal exchange between staying and leaving members.

Leaving members of the Two Leave groups reported forming an alliance with each other during the earliest parts of the group's task work. Staying participants stated that the leaving members were hostile in their insistence about contributing to the group. One of the Two Leave alliances actually convinced themselves that they had not been asked to leave. They vehemently argued that no one would be asked to leave if the group performed well together.

All Leave participants reported that they did not talk about their separation. During the task discussion period, one group decided to discuss the planning of a class party for the end of the semester. All Leave group members discussed a future, and therefore somewhat safer separation than the immediate separation indicated in the simulation.

Others Leave members indicated that they were briefly concerned about their personal security. They reported that after reassuring one another of their safety, they directly discussed the dilemma they faced in working through their task: Should they be advocates for those leaving, or should they be concerned with the future of the company?

Finally, Control group members reported that they had a brief task discussion absent of conflict and dilemma. After the task discussion it was observed that the Control groups spent a short period of time praising their effectiveness. One group then spent time trying to "figure out" the purposes behind the exercise, another discussed unrelated activities such as television programs. Some Control group members said that after listening to the experiences of people in other conditions they felt short changed by the simulation because they did not have a high level of emotional arousal.

On the whole, the qualitative data were supportive of the statistical results. The simulation participants generally described having different experiences depending on which group they belonged to and whether they were a staying or leaving member. Chapter 6 explores how the results fit expectations and can be understood using theory.

NOTES

1. "In depth" meant that more than one page was devoted to separation anxiety. Generally, the effects of separation anxiety and personal historical factors which contribute to separation anxiety were discussed.

2. "In depth" meant that more than one page was devoted to the simulation.

3. The Collared Exercise (Herbert & Astrachan, 1988) was an intergroup exercise given earlier in the semester in which the class was split into two groups: oppressors and oppressed.

6

Separation Anxiety, Behavior, and Emotions During the Simulation

The simulated world created for studying mergers, acquisitions, and separation anxiety produced feelings and behaviors similar to those reported by people who have experienced merger announcements first-hand. Workers were profoundly affected by the announcement of a merger in both cases. In the simulation, this was confirmed by multiple statistical tests including Multiple Analysis of Variance contrast tests and repeated measures Analysis of Variance for the main and interaction effects.

The number of people leaving and remaining influenced attitudes and affect. Further, people behaved differently in their groups depending on the number of people separating. Prior to this research, the impact of the number of people leaving was unrecognized in the din of veritable mergers and acquisitions. These effects were investigated by exploring the Multiple Analysis of Variance interaction effect contrasts, charts of the Analytical Condition means, and qualitative reports.

This chapter is devoted to explaining how the above findings and other, more detailed conclusions were reached. It proceeds in five segments. The first answers the question, "What were the similarities among all groups?"' This section looks at how people responded to the entire simulation regardless of how many people were leaving the group. The second explores the question, "How were people affected by the merger news?" This section investigates immediate responses to merger news for all groups and how initial reactions were shaped by the number of members leaving. The third section addresses the question, "How did separation anxiety, in combination with the number of people leaving and staying, affect behavior in the group?" This part looks at both how people behaved and how interactions in the group further changed attitudes and feelings. In this section, Analytical Conditions are examined one at a time. The fourth piece investigates the question, "What were the differences between the three simulation runs: Yale 1987, Michigan State 1988, and Yale 1988?" The purpose of this segment was to both determine if there were other issues which influenced reactions during the simulation and to demonstrate that the findings hold in different settings with different types of people. Finally, the fifth section provides conclusions from the simulation results. A model of how mergers and acquisitions affect feelings, attitudes, and behavior is a fundamental conclusion.

SIMILARITIES AMONG GROUPS

Similarities among all Analytical Conditions are revealed by the main Period effect. A statistically significant main effect indicates some similarity across all groups. The Period effect was significant in 28 of the 31 (90 percent) items and for both the scales shown in Table 5. This indicates that the average participant changed over the course of the simulation.

The significance of the main Period effect does not imply that the Control or any other specific group changed over time. It holds that on average, simulation participants changed over time. This is important because Control group members are a primary comparison group. If they displayed a pattern similar to other groups, it would imply that something not intentionally in the simulation design accounted for the reported effects. Figures 4 through 10 provide a preliminary indication that the simulation produced foreseen effects. Those figures reveal that Control group members did not experience dramatic changes over the course of the simulation.

The independent examination of the Control group members and the comparison of them with members from the other groups displayed in Table 7, show that Control group members changed over the course of the simulation in terms of the Group Characteristics Scale and the Work Quality item. However, they did not exhibit any changes in the Emotion Scale. In contrast, all other Analytical Conditions show a significant Period effect for the Emotion Scale. Control group members did not experience any emotional effects of the simulation, while all other participants did.

The merger news and separation information had a distinct emotional effect while other information did not. Further analyses, discussed below, reveal differences between Control group members and members from other Analytical Conditions. Specifically, although Control group members were affected by the simulation along one scale, they were affected differently from members in other Analytical Conditions. The qualitative data, especially the reports from Control group members, support this conclusion.

That Control group members were not affected emotionally is especially important because it indicates that they did not experience separation anxiety.

Generally we would expect to see separation anxiety most clearly in short term emotional changes - before interaction occurs. That members of other groups were affected emotionally supports the idea that the merger news evoked separation anxiety.

The large percentage of significant Period by Analytical Condition interaction effects shown in Table 5 indicates that individuals were affected by the different numbers of people separating from their groups. A quick glance at Figures 4 through 10 adds confirmation. The specifics of how they were differently affected is detailed below.

In general, it is clear that the simulation affected all groups except the Control. The Control group was not at all affected emotionally and was affected differently than the other Analytical Conditions with regard to the Group Characteristics Scale and the Work Quality item. This substantiates the first hypothesis: Separation anxiety was stimulated by the announcement of the imminent departure of one or more members from a group, or one or more groups from an organization.

EFFECTS OF MERGER NEWS

The effect of the merger news is seen in how people changed from Period 3 to Period 4. This represents the change from before receiving the merger news to immediately after reading about the merger. The statistical tests used for measuring this change were MANOVA contrast tests. Shown in Table 6, the contrasts between Periods 3 and 4 reveal that the Emotion Scale and two of the five item main effect contrasts were significant. This is confirmed in Figure 4 by a downward shift from Period 3 to Period 4 in the Emotion Scale chart displayed by nearly all groups. The Control group displayed a slight, insignificant, downward shift from Period 3 to Period 4 in the Emotion Scale chart.

Table 8 shows that in addition to the Control group, two other Analytical Conditions did not have a significant change in the Emotion Scale from Period 3 to Period 4. These were staying members of the One Leaves group and All Leave group members. However, the interaction effects displayed in Table 7 suggest that these two Analytical Conditions were different than the Control group in the Emotion Scale. Because Control group members did not have any information about a merger or separation, the downward trends for the other conditions indicate that the merger and separation information affected the other Analytical Conditions. Even without group discussion, the merger news had an immediate negative emotional effect on all but Control group members. This lends further support for the first hypothesis.

As well as affecting all but the Control group members, there is evidence which substantiates the idea that people responded differently to the merger news based on the number of people leaving the groups. Such differences are revealed by the MANOVA interaction effect contrasts of Period 3 with Period 4 displayed in Table 6. This interaction effect indicates that people responded to the merger news differently based on the number of people leaving the group. The Emotion Scale and two of the five item interaction effect contrasts were significant. This shows that there was a difference, at least at the emotional level, in the immediate impact of the separation information. Examination of Figure 4, the Emotion Scale chart, confirms this finding. This chart displays three categories of responses. First, as discussed above, Control group members were the least affected. Second, moderately affected were those told that separation would occur, yet who were not anticipating leaving the group themselves—All Leave, Others Leave, and staying members of the One Leaves and Two Leave groups. Third, the most negatively affected were the leaving members of groups where one or more members were told that they would be leaving while the others remained—leaving members of the One Leaves and Two Leave groups.

Others and All Leave Groups

Others Leave group members had very slight initial responses to the merger news. The Period by Condition interaction effect of Table 7 shows that they did have some differences with the Control group but it is not clear that this was solely a result of the merger news. The MANOVA contrasts of Table 8 showed that they did feel differently and held different attitudes about their group after reading about the merger. Figures 4 through 10 confirm these tests. It is evident that Others Leave members experienced separation anxiety. However, they were only marginally affected because their situation posed minor threat, none of their group was leaving, they shared their status with all members of the group, and a boundary did not form within the group. The experiences of the Others Leave members confirms part of the fifth hypothesis: Separation anxiety was stimulated in groups where all members expected to stay yet others in their organization were going to leave.

Members of the All Leave group reported that they were not dramatically affected by the merger news. This was evidenced in the qualitative data and in the lack of any significant MANOVA contrasts between Periods 3 and 4 shown in Table 8. The All Leave members were in a very psychologically threatening situation because they received signals that they would all separate. Somewhat ironically, because everyone in the group expects to leave, this condition provides the largest opportunity for psychosocial support. Experiencing separation from the same perspective left little reason for individuals to feel left-out of the group. While they ultimately faced separation, they did so together, having no merger caused boundaries that cleaved the group. Indeed, the separation announcement added another shared feature: the same ignominious fate.

The All Leave group members were able to use the group to defend against separation anxiety. This is similar to Jaques' (1974) notion of using groups and organizations to defend against anxiety. Observation and feedback from participants supported this interpretation. One member of an All Leave group reported that he "felt closer to the group members than at any other time during the semester." The results for similar groups occurring in natural settings would likely be different. Interaction within the workplace would reduce the ability to deny the impending separation because of the presence of multiple communications, symbols, and other reminders of upcoming departure.

These results further support the first hypothesis and also support part of the second hypotheses: A small increase in distress was found for groups in which the entire group shared the same status as leaving group members.

One Leaves and Two Leave Groups

The increasingly negative emotions displayed in Figure 4 show that leaving members, expecting to be isolated and generally left-out of their groups, had larger negative reactions than staying members. This is confirmed by Figure 8, Feel Left-Out Item Chart, which displays the leaving members of the One Leaves and Two Leave groups feeling highly left-out just before group interaction. Leaving members felt left-out before remaining members had any opportunity to behave in ways that isolated them.

Leaving members of the Two Leave group had an additional fear which may have contributed to their negative change in the Emotion Scale. At Period 4, the two leaving members had not yet formed an alliance. Each separating individual was prone to wonder whether the other would be supportive. Separating members may have feared that they would be "played off" against one another. They may have anticipated being slighted, sacrificed, and otherwise used in a political fashion by the other separating person in order to gain favor with the remaining group members. Fearing a zero-sum game, in which one member wins at the expense of the other, is similar to the initial context presented by the Prisoner's Dilemma experiments (Axlerod & Hamilton, 1981). Similarly, they found that without the opportunity for interaction and with the consequence being separation, people anticipate competition. In those experiments, the magnitude of separation was to be separated from society.

The Emotion Scale Chart (Figure 4) further depicts the adverse effects of merger news on the remaining members of groups where separation was to occur. These groups faced boundary disruption. Rather than feeling happy about being spared personal separation from the group, remaining group members felt somewhat worse off because of the merger news. This is consistent with the idea of survivor guilt experienced by survivors of accidents and tragedies. However, there was little evidence of guilt reported by staying members. This could be due to the fact that the leaving members did not actually leave during the simulation. So while some evidence of guilt was seen prior to separation, it may be that substantial guilt feelings only occur after separation.

In general, the results support the first hypothesis: Separation anxiety was caused by the announcement of the imminent departure of one or more members from a group, or one or more groups from an organization. Further, the differences that were accounted for by the numbers of individuals leaving constructed a foundation for different patterns of intragroup interaction (group process) predicted by the remaining hypotheses. Finally, the small amount of change displayed by the Control group in Figures 4 through 10 and in Table 8 indicates that without the merger news, the simulation did not cause detectable anxiety.

ANXIETY, NUMBERS LEAVING, AND GROUP PROCESS

One of the most important aspects of this research was the exploration of how separation anxiety interacts with different numbers of people leaving to produce different patterns of behavior. It was seen above that the initial response to merger news was different based on the number leaving a group. This section explores how initial responses get translated into behavior which can become self-perpetuating.

To gauge the effect of separation anxiety on group process the difference between what happened before group process was allowed to occur (Period 4) with what happened afterwards (Period 5) was examined. Because there was no new intervention introduced between Periods 4 and 5, significant MANOVA contrasts between Periods 4 and 5 reflect the consequences of group process. Table 6 shows a significant MANOVA contrast test between Periods 4 and 5 for the Emotion Scale. This indicates that emotions changed due to the way people were interacting in their groups.

Table 6 also indicates that the Group Characteristics Scale interaction effect contrast of Period 4 with Period 5 was significant. This suggests that behavior was dependent on the number of members staying in and leaving each group. The feedback and observational data indicate that group process, feelings, and opinions were intimately linked. Specific behavior patterns and their effects are discussed below for each Analytical Condition.

All Leave Condition

Within the All Leave and Others Leave groups, members shared the same position. For the All Leave members, this provided the ability to deny thoughts and feelings born of separation anxiety. This is supported by qualitative and quantitative materials. Table 8 reveals that they displayed no significant changes from Period 4 to Period 5. This is partly due to the small number of participants in the All Leave condition. Figures 4 through 10 illustrate changes from Period 3 to Period 5 indicating that they were affected by the merger news and group interactions. For example, Figure 4 shows that they had a negative emotional reaction following the merger announcement. The negative change was followed by a fairly strong positive change in the Emotion Scale. This indicates that something happened which improved their emotional state.

One explanation for the displayed pattern of a negative then positive change in emotions is that group member interactions enabled them to deny the negative affect experienced earlier. The qualitative data suggests that their improved emotional state was not due to their having accepted or even acknowledged their oncoming separation. Further, the questions asked after the simulation—Tables 9 and 10—clearly show the denial displayed by the All Leave members in their failure to identify the major issues underlying the simulation as either individual or group separation and in that they did not want to discuss issues concerning leaving members.

Along with the leaving members of the One Leaves groups, All Leave members were the least happy with their company's superiors. This is an interesting finding for the All Leavers because the other measures of affect indicated that they were relatively positive. Unhappiness with company superiors can be interpreted as an intergroup projection. Negative feelings felt within the group were believed to be the result of outside forces and were expressed as anger toward superiors.

Rather than create divisions within the All Leave groups, it seems that people behaved in ways that increased group boundary strength. Because all members faced the same threat and shared the same status as leavers, group members drew closer together. For example, participants displayed a sharp decrease in how much they felt left out. Figure 8 indicates a strong group process influence.

Even though they felt included and social emotional support was abundantly available, people reported that discussion concerning personal separation was difficult to initiate. Such discussion would cause them to confront the immediate source of their anxiety and was therefore avoided. In other words, no one in the groups felt comfortable in engaging the topic of the merger and the upcoming dismemberment of their group. This implies that social emotional support will only ameliorate the consequences of separation anxiety if people are willing to provide that support.

While All Leave members may have pulled together to defend against separation anxiety, Figure 7 shows that they actually liked their group less after interacting. This may represent a reaction to feeling confined by the increased strength of their boundary or an attempt to reduce the negative impact of the upcoming separation in a self protective "sour grapes" or "I'm glad we're parting, I didn't like them any more anyway" form. Similar to Klein's (1948) concepts of depressive and persecutory anxiety, it is also possible that they liked their group less because they believed that it was a bad group. This can happen through a processes of internalization (Aronfreed, 1969) or the resolution of cognitive dissonance (Festinger, 1957) in which they came to believe that their group was bad because they had all been asked to leave. The time they spent on their task, which is one measure of performance, invariably suffered as a result.

In general, the results supported the second hypothesis: In groups where separation anxiety was stimulated and all group members shared the same status as leavers, a small increase in distress was followed by the establishment of an insulating boundary around the entire group. As a result of the activation of denial and protective mechanisms, group members did not show additional increase in distress. In fact, All Leave group members reported a marked reduction in negative affect and an overall increase in their positive view of their group.

The results from the All Leave group might differ from naturally occurring All Leave type groups. In on-going organizations it is likely that their interaction with other members of the organization would add complexity to their emotional and behavioral reactions. For example, if only one group of several was leaving, the situation would have elements of a One Leaves type group, with members being more likely to feel depressed and withdrawn. This would, of course, depend on a number of factors including the group's pre-existing boundary strength.

Others Leave Condition

Like the All Leave groups' members, members of the Others Leave groups shared a similar status: They were staying in the group and organization. Figures 4, 5, and 6 show the Others Leave group members reporting an initial decrease in the Emotion Scale, Group Characteristics Scale, and the Work Quality item. This was followed by a large positive rebound indicative of the powerful effects of group interaction. Table 8 shows that for both the Emotion Scale and the Work Quality item there was a significant positive change from before the merger news to the end of the simulation. As shown in Table 10, these positive increases were not due to the activation of denial mechanisms. Others Leave group members were not reluctant to identify the major issues that they were dealing with during the simulation as being due to group or individual separation. They also did not report being very angry with their company's superiors. This indicates that they did not engage in splitting and projection. Members also reported that they had a relatively balanced discussion of the issues affecting staying and leaving members of their organization. Figure 8 displays that they did not feel very left out of their group at the end of the simulation which further shows that they did not interact in a manner that internally separated the group.

Others Leave group members' responses to the post-simulation questions tended toward the middle. The two exceptions were that they believed they did not participate more than other members of their group and they thought that their group would have made different question choices if they had not been a member of their group. These responses are consistent with the view that separation anxiety stimulated in the Others Leave groups facilitated a discussion of both the staying and leaving aspects of their situation. The absence of a schism in the group prevented the development of any internal boundary or obstacle to such discussion. Observations and their reports indicated that they spent most of the simulation working productively on the task.

In general, the results for the Others Leave group support the fifth hypothesis: In groups where separation anxiety was stimulated, yet all group members expected to stay (e.g. others in their organization were expected to leave), members identified with both the remaining and leaving members of their organization. Both sides of the issue, leaving and remaining, could therefore be discussed within the group. However, like the All Leave group, similar groups occurring in natural settings might react differently. Coming into direct contact with leaving groups and members of the organization would increase the emotional stress associated with being a staying member of the organization. Increased stress increases the need to deny, repress, and otherwise avoid negative and painful emotions. Increased stress also fosters the over emphasis and over valuation of positive emotions. This would make a "real-life" Others Leave type situation analogous to that experienced by the staying members of either the One Leaves or Two Leave groups.

One Leaves Leaving Members Condition

The One Leaves and Two Leave groups represent a special case because they had both leaving and staying members. It was predicted that in these situations a boundary would form between those staying and leaving. Further, quite different and intense feelings and behavior are generally evidenced on each side of such a boundary. The most dramatic negative impact of group behavior was reported by leaving members in the One Leaves groups. For example, in the Feel Left-Out Chart (Figure 8) nearly every other Analytical Condition felt less left-out in Period 5, after group interaction. Yet, leaving members of the One Leaves groups felt extremely left-out. The merger news and group process resulted in their feeling isolated and separate without ever having left the group. They experienced the group boundary as having been redefined to exclude them. Having no one to share their leaving status they had no choice but to cope with anxiety alone. This analysis is overwhelmingly supported by qualitative data.

The post-simulation questionnaire items further support the view that the One Leaves groups' leaving members felt isolated and outside of the group boundary. They identified the major issue occurring during the simulation as one of group separation, believed that one question was chosen to satisfy them, and more than any other groups' members, reported that they wanted to discuss issues concerning leaving members far more than the rest of their group. These data strongly suggest that the leaving members of the One Leaves groups powerfully felt the effects of being excluded from their group. They also reported feeling less close to their group after the simulation which again indicates that they felt cut out of their groups. A boundary quickly formed around the staying group members which served to exclude the leaving member.

Leaving members did not see all of the bad behavior as coming from their staying group members. Leaving members were the least happy with their company's superiors, which suggests projection. Negative feelings experienced within the group were seen by the leaving group members as in part resulting from outside the group. Leaving member projection may represent a way of coping with their inconsistent desire to remain attached to their group in the face of their group's attempts to exclude them. Some of the anger expressed for their superiors may have helped to redirect emotions felt about their group. However, because of their separate position within the group they could not displace all of their negative feelings and consequently they reported feeling quite negatively at the end of the simulation. Further, displays of open hostility toward group members would risk their prematurely being ejected from their group. Therefore, showing anger would require them to feel comfortable about leaving the group.

In general, experiences of the leaving members of the One Leaves groups support Hypotheses 3, 4, and 4a: Group process apparently led to the formation of a boundary that excluded the leaving member; group process was affected by the number of leaving members—one; and the leaving member, who was in an isolated position, experienced high levels of distress, tended to withdraw from the group, and felt negatively about the group's work and its members. In organizational settings people in this type of isolated condition could be expected to experience an even worse situation in part because their group members could more easily avoid interacting with them.

One Leaves Staying Members Condition

Staying members of the One Leaves groups had widely divergent experiences from their leaving counterparts. They provided even more evidence that a boundary formed between staying and leaving members. For example, the Group Characteristics Scale Chart (Figure 5) shows that while the leaving members became more negative in their view of their group, staying members reported a slight, nonsignificant increase in their view of their group. They tended to believe that their group functioned better after the merger news and group interaction. They held this view even though they participated in excluding their leaving members.

Figure 9 (Feel Sad Chart) is important because it displays a zigzag pattern for the staying members of the One Leaves group. When they first read the merger news they reported a large increase in feeling sad. Yet, from Period 4 to Period 5 they demonstrated a large decrease in feeling sad. This indicates that somehow they alleviated their negative feelings. Again, as a result of group process, the staying members successfully denied their negative feelings. Further evidence of denial is shown in Table 10. Those staying wanted to discuss issues concerning the leaving group member far less than those leaving.

They did not project their negative feelings onto their company's superiors. They were happy with their company's superiors. They did not need to use the company's superiors as an object on which to project their negative emotions because they had a readily available object within their group—the leaving member. Projecting negative emotions onto the leaving— member further helped staying members deny their own separation-related feelings and anxiety. It seems that staying members could dismiss the input of leaving participants and in the process continue to isolate the leaving member.

The qualitative reports show that some staying members consciously intended to protect, or at least not hurt, the feelings of the leaving member by not talking about them. However, not discussing the separation and talking about issues that affected the remaining members served to further isolate the leaving member. In addition, it also worked to protect staying members from feeling negatively. This is a phenomenon akin to closing ones eyes during a frightening situation.

Regardless of the intentions of the staying members, a schism developed in the One Leaves groups. Some of the actions of the staying members, while perhaps intended to ease discomfort and include the leaving member, actually served to both highlight and deny differences. By not talking about the problem staying members communicated that they felt the problem was not important, while leaving members felt ever more isolated.

The qualitative data indicated that while many staying members made conjectures about leaving members' feelings, there was little explicit discussion of emotions and attitudes. This is striking and suggests how powerful the anxiety was given that they had to fill out a questionnaire which took an inventory of their emotional state approximately every 15 minutes, were participants in a course that stressed open communication about emotions, and had all formulated psychological contracts that stressed openness, honesty, and commitment to the group.

In general, the results of the One Leaves groups' staying members support Hypotheses 3, 4, and 4a: An internal boundary formed which excluded the leaving member as was evident in the widely different views of staying and leaving members; group process was affected by the number of leaving members; and after an initial negative emotional change, staying members felt fairly positively about their group and their emotional state, suggesting a denial of their separation anxiety related negative feelings. In organizational settings where one member is to leave a group staying members would likely find it even easier to exclude the leaving member. Others staying in the organization could be expected to support denial and to not call attention to the imminent departure of leaving members. Likewise, staying members have many opportunities to avoid the presence of a leaving coworker.

Two Leave Leaving Members Condition

Similar to the One Leaves groups, members in the Two Leave groups reported reacting differently based on whether they were staying or leaving their group. Overall, while they felt badly after receiving the merger news, leaving members of the Two Leave groups felt better following group interaction. This rebound occurred after they had time to form an alliance and establish an internal boundary. Having at least one other member with which to share their experience enabled leaving members to deny and fight separation and to feel less lonely.

Table 10 shows that after the simulation leaving members reported participating more than the staying members. Consistent with this finding is that staying members reported participating less than the leaving members. By having another leaving member with which to share their emotional state and views, the two leaving members gained enough strength and emotional support to attempt to influence their groups. In agreement with this interpretation are the results of the items: Felt closer to the group after the simulation ended; No single strong alliance formed; I teamed up with one other group member; and I wanted to discuss issues concerning leaving group members far more than the rest of the group. It appears that a boundary formed around the leaving members, empowering them to interact with those staying. Qualitative data, especially reports from staying members, also indicate that the leaving members formed an alliance that enabled them to fight exclusion.

In general, the results of the Two Leave groups' leaving members support Hypotheses 3, 4, and 4b: An internal boundary formed which separated the staying and leaving members and after an initial period of separation, the staying and leaving members interacted in a manner that brought the entire group closer together with a greater sharing of views at the end of the simulation. The situation of the leaving members was similar to those in the

All Leave condition in that they shared the same status. However, because they interacted with the staying members in their group they were less willing to passively deny their circumstances and actively fought to feel included in the group.

Two Leave Staying Members Condition

The staying members of the Two Leave group initially had an interest in forming an intragroup boundary which would allow them to exclude those leaving. However, due to the persistence of the leaving members, those staying could not entirely disregard leaving members' views. This resulted in the development of a shared view between staying and leaving members displayed in their convergent trend from Period 4 to Period 5. For example, the Work Quality Item Chart (Figure 6) shows them reporting similarly after the simulation, suggesting that active communication occurring within the group led to similar views of their work quality. Efforts to resolve differences and compromise left them feeling they performed well. This suggests that in the context of separation, group discussion can have a unifying and empowering effect.

Leaving and staying members of the Two Leave groups differed significantly in terms of how much they participated in their group and how much they wanted to discuss issues concerning leaving members. Even more than the One Leave groups' staying members, the Two Leave groups' staying members reported that the majority of their group did want to discuss issues concerning leaving group members. While they wanted to deny the effects of having leaving members (e.g., individually they reported that they wanted to discuss issues concerning their leaving group members the least), having a larger proportion of the group leaving made avoidance and suppression less possible.

In sum, the results of the Two Leave groups' staying members support Hypotheses 3, 4, and 4b: As was seen with the leaving members, an internal boundary formed which separated the staying and leaving members, and after group interaction the staying and leaving members were closer together, felt better, and held more similar views than prior to group discussion. Like the staying members of the One Leaves group, in organizational settings staying members of Two Leave type groups would likely find it easier to avoid leaving members. This could help them to disregard the leaving members and subsequently not develop a shared view in the group.

Control Condition

It was expected that Control group members would not report any large changes due to interaction in the group because separation anxiety was not evoked. Figures 4 through 10 show that the Control group members were little changed from Period 4 to Period 5, indicating that they were not influenced greatly by any unintended effects of the simulation. The responses of the Control group members to the post-simulation questions indicate that the group did not feel anxious and that behavior was unaffected by any extenuating circumstances. According to Table 10, they had a high level of participation, a low belief that they made a unique contribution, a low level of teaming up within their groups, and they were happiest with their superiors.

One unanticipated finding is that they identified individual separation as a major underlying issue. This may be due to the disbandment of the groups at the end of the simulation which occurred shortly before these questions were answered. As shown in Figure 8, with the exception of the Control group, all other Analytical Conditions reported liking the group less after the simulation. Because separation anxiety was stimulated in all but the Control group, this implies that liking the group is related to separation anxiety. The stimulation of separation anxiety during the simulation makes separation at the end of the simulation a relatively more intense emotional issue. In general, the responses of the Control group members do not contradict any of the hypotheses of this research.

DIFFERENCES BETWEEN SIMULATION RUNS

Understanding the differences between simulation runs can both show the veracity of the findings and provide new insights into the effects of mergers, acquisitions, and separation anxiety. Naturally occurring differences between runs can illuminate important additional factors that influence separation anxiety, emotions, and behavior.

The participants from Yale University reported greater transitions distress than did those from Michigan State University. One possible interpretation consistent with the theory of adult development (Levinson et al., 1978) is that Yale University students were at an age where issues of separation are critical. The period encompassing the early twenties is characterized by separating from parents, family of origin, and one's preadult life structure. While the stage of adult development may have affected transitions distress scores, the correlation between age and the Transitions Distress Scale was close to zero and was not significant. In fact, the correlation was slightly positive, indicating that the older one is the more separations are experienced as stressful.

Other factors which may have influenced transitions distress scores include personality, culture, prior experience with stressful transitions, and the presence of other stressors. For example, Yale and the northeast may be a more stressful setting than Michigan State and the midwest. There may also be some correlate of personality which affects transitions distress. Likewise, there may be some cultural predispositions around transitions which differed for the east coast and midwestern students.

The comparisons shown in Table 3 indicate that people experienced the simulation differently based on the setting. However, when the Transitions Distress Scale was included in the analyses as a variable, as shown in Table 4, differences between the runs decreased. This shows that differences between the settings can be accounted for by the differences in participants' reported transitions distress. However, there were still several interaction effects which were significant that included the Run term. This implies that there are additional factors that account for differences in the simulation settings. These differences could include differences in the course content, course process (e.g., the Yale course had a greater emphasis on self-reflection), the authority of the researcher (e.g., in the midwest the researcher was a guest instructor and in the northeast a teacher) and teaching staff as well as other differences mentioned above. It is important to note that even though there were differences between the settings the hypotheses were still supported. The consistency of findings across the replications provides evidence for the powerful impact of separation anxiety.

SUMMARY

The hypotheses were well supported.

Separation anxiety was stimulated in groups that received merger news.

Intragroup boundaries formed in groups that contained both staying and leaving members. Staying and leaving members had different experiences.

Group process was affected by the number of staying and leaving members.

- In the One Leaves groups, leaving members reported feeling isolated and high levels of distress while staying members reported low levels of discomfort.
- In the Two Leave groups, leaving members initially felt isolated and then formed alliances which allowed them to have a substantial impact on their groups. Staying members reported moderate discomfort and engaged leaving members in discussion.
- In the All Leave groups, members apparently denied the emotional impact of the upcoming separation. Though they reported not being affected negatively, they displayed self-protective behavior in that they liked their groups less after the simulation.
- The Others Leave group members responded in a manner which suggests that intragroup boundaries did not impede group discussion.
- Finally, Control group members reported behavior which is consistent with groups operating without anxiety in a nonthreatening environment.

CONCLUSIONS

The theory of separation anxiety and the results from the mergers and acquisition simulation suggest the model displayed in Figure 11. The model holds that mergers and acquisitions raise separation anxiety which, in turn, influences individual feelings and behavior. These affect the patterns of group behavior which also exert an influence on individual feelings and behavior. This reciprocal influence can set up self-perpetuating patterns of behavior. The patterns of behavior are intimately connected with the task-related performance by the group. The number of people leaving and staying in the group affects the intensity of separation anxiety experienced, individual feelings and behavior, and patterns of group behavior. Finally, prior separation experiences influence the intensity of separation anxiety experienced. One of the more important aspects of the model addressed in this research are the multiple effects of the number of people leaving and staying. The details of the theory and results provide more insight into how the number of people leaving and staying affects separation anxiety, individual feelings and behavior, and patterns of group behavior.

The experiment clearly demonstrated that simulated mergers and acquisitions increase separation anxiety. The effects of separation anxiety on individuals and groups depended upon the number of people leaving and separating from the group. In situations where one person was leaving a group, the individual had a strong emotional response characterized by increased sadness and withdrawal. The remaining members of the group quickly reformed their group boundary to exclude the leaving member. Further, they acted in ways which exposed their denial of the separation, or at least their desire to not talk about their colleague's departure. In groups where more than one person was leaving, the leaving members formed an

Figure 11
Model of Effects of Mergers and Acquisitions

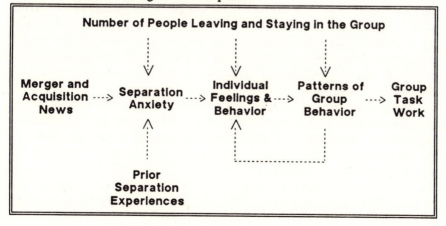

alliance and attempted to resist exclusion. Denial of the impending separation was characteristic of groups where members perceived that everyone was leaving. When group members were aware that others within their organization were leaving, some separation anxiety was stimulated. However, they were able to discuss the separation of others in a relatively amicable environment. Separation anxiety also resulted in attempts to secure and intensify bonds which made the separation experience more emotionally stressful.

According to participant reports, prior separation experiences greatly influenced responses to separation anxiety. Most notably, prior separations that had a traumatic quality were related to more disturbing emotional responses to subsequent separations. Common previous separations that reportedly had a strong impact included divorce or separation of parents, death of parents, death of a sibling, death of a child, and one's own divorce or separation. These are consistent with Hamburg's (1969) 20 universal stressful situations.[1]

Observations and feedback also suggested that separations can be managed, reducing the intensity of separation anxiety and its negative effects and emphasizing positive aspects. Especially when guided, people demonstrated the capacity to learn from their experiences and to develop more functional ways of coping with them and preparing for future separations.

The strong effects noted for the simulation experience and everyday life experiences are quite strong given the limited life experiences of the participants in this study. Adults with greater life experience would likely yield more evocative and powerful results as their greater history and attachments combines with separation anxiety to shape emotions and behavior.

While the results were quite definitive, there are arguable difficulties with the ability to apply these findings to naturally occurring groups. The simulated groups were without a predefined structure, the attachment period was relatively short, and the circumstances surrounding the separation were simplified. We would generally expect that the relatively short attachment building period, in comparison with "naturally occurring" situations, would not yield a high degree of separation anxiety nor as many significant results. Some more fundamental emotional issue was tapped into merely by the suggestion of member separation. The reduced complexity and attachment period should have worked to minimize separation anxiety and make the results more conservative.

The groups were not set up with a defined structure. Naturally occurring groups often form with a leader or pivotal member who is the primary object of individual attachment to the group. We might expect to find other behavior patterns when a pivotal person is separating. For example, we might see acting out behavior such as ignoring instructions or aggression toward authority figures, unacknowledged and recognized infighting, and massive failure. These behaviors reflect the belief that the group will cease if the pivotal member departs. The simulation also did not allow for individuals and groups to interact in a larger system. It is possible that additional behavioral responses would be seen in a larger system. For example, attachments to others might be strengthened or weakened as a response to separation in the work group.

It is important to note that the simulation was designed to examine separation anxiety in groups whose life was less than 90 minutes. While these findings would still apply, longer-lived groups might experience added complexity and intensity. Over a longer period of time different patterns of behavioral and emotional reactions may occur. It may be that all the emotional reactions described here would emerge and overlap. Jacobs et al. (1987-88) discovered such evolving patterns when studying individual loss reactions.

Some may argue that separation anxiety is an unimportant factor in real life separations. Self-reflective thinkers know how painful and traumatic separation experiences can be regardless of circumstance. For example, even desired separations, such as the planned termination of a marriage, often has a profound impact (cf. Weiss, 1975; Marris, 1974). Trivial separation cues, such as seeing your loved one interact with a stranger or events which mark the aging of your children, elicit strong emotional responses. While circumstances serve to limit or expand the ways with which anxiety is coped, they do not eliminate anxiety. They only influence the way in which it is expressed. There may be circumstances in which separation anxiety is actively managed. In such cases, while anxiety may persist, its recognition, acknowledgment, and active management allows more pleasant and beneficial aspects of separation to flourish. Issues involved in the management of separation anxiety and how it is manifest in situations other than mergers and acquisitions is a concern of Chapter 7.

NOTE

1. Hamburg's (1969) 20 universal stressful situations are:

1. separation from parents in childhood;
2. displacement by siblings;
3. childhood experiences of rejection;
4. illness and injuries in childhood;
5. illness and death of parents;
6. severe illness and injuries of the adult years;
7. the initial transition from home to school;
8. puberty;
9. later school transitions;
10. competitive graduate education;

11. marriage;
12. pregnancy;
13. menopause;
14. necessity for periodic moves to a new environment;
15. retirement;
16. rapid technological and social change;
17. wars and threats of wars;
18. migration;
19. acculturation;
20. social mobility.

7

Separation Anxiety in Everyday Life: Implications

How might theory and research findings be applied to real-world incidents? The answer to this question has three parts. First, because separation anxiety is central to mergers, acquisitions, and other organizational transitions and because the theory of separation anxiety is far from complete, added critical issues are explored. This takes place in a speculative discussion of questions and research issues that are important for further consideration. In addition to the theory and examples already presented, this discussion will strengthen knowledge needed for the accurate detection and appropriate management of separation anxiety. This section briefly connects many of these basic issues with managing separation anxiety in the work place.

The second issue covered in an effort to develop practical applications of this work are general instances of separation anxiety. Such occasions concern nonmanagerial relationships such as family, close friends, and intergroup relationships in general. Witnessing how separation anxiety works in these situations provides background for understanding its effects in managerial relationships. Often, separation anxiety is more clearly seen in nonmanagerial relationships because of the relative strength of attachments to family and close friends.

With future issues and nonmanagerial relations explored, practical implications of how one might detect and manage separation anxiety can be made. This is particularly important for organizations that are vulnerable to separation anxiety such as hospitals, schools, or other organizations that have a significant proportion of transient membership, family owned or controlled firms, and other organizations that have well defined membership such as military, law enforcement, and other organizations that exist in an environment of high danger, as well as organizations under threat of mergers and acquisitions.

FURTHER CRITICAL ISSUES

There are at least five areas that need further consideration for a thorough understanding of separation anxiety and its dynamics. The first regards the basic mechanism of separation anxiety at the individual level. This addresses the question, "Why do we get anxious around separations?" Closely related to the first area are the effects of prior separation experiences. For example, "Do prior traumatic separations influence subsequent anxiety?" The third concerns the effects of the settings in which separation anxiety occurs. This area addresses issues such as the atmosphere and culture in which relationships exist. The fourth area involves the level (e.g., individual, group, organizational) at which the effects of separation anxiety are explored. This concerns two questions: "What level is separating—is it an individual, a group, or an organization?" And, "Is the impact of the separation different for each level?" Finally, the fifth area comprises specific characteristics of the anticipated separation. This involves items such as the expected time until separation, the directness and clarity of the separation communication, the intensity or importance of the separation, and the degree to which the separation is desired. These components are always present in all separation experiences and potentially exert a great influence on how anxiety is displayed in behavior.

Basic Mechanism of Separation Anxiety

The basic separation anxiety mechanism is likely the most difficult to explore. An approach that may hold promise is the relationship of separation anxiety to the process of habituation and withdrawal. We can conjecture that the process of getting used to something is an active process. The presence of something we are attached to may affect us at a neurochemical level. The absence and anticipated absence of the expected may cause actual withdrawal-like reactions. This implies that minimizing withdrawal is an important feature of managing separation. For example, withdrawal symptoms can be eased through a weaning or gradual disaccustoming process.

An area related to withdrawal processes is the idea that our memory and thought processes are intimately connected to our environment. Objects and people within the environment serve to trigger and help recollect memories. The anticipated loss of such objects may be accompanied by feelings that we are losing a part of our past and a part of ourselves. Anticipated loss of others may actually be experienced as the anticipated loss of parts of the self. To compensate for this a substitute mechanism for aiding memory may need to be employed; for example, a written diary or some other log of the relationship.

Prior Separation Experiences

Historical separation experiences can be studied at three levels: individual, group, and organizational. This book has addressed some issues concerning the impact of prior individual experiences. For example, it was strongly suggested that previous traumatic experiences increase the emotionality of later separations. Prior traumatic separations can also reduce the desire to make new attachments in an effort to avoid being hurt again. This reaction can have unhappy consequences for people working in vocations that require high levels of communication and "networking." It was also suggested that personal behavior patterns for coping with separation develop from prior experiences; for example, anger and conflict, withdrawal and detachment, and denial and avoidance. While situational factors limit and shape long term reactions to separation, pre-existing coping behaviors may act as first responses to separation anxiety.

These behaviors are difficult to recognize for the trained specialist, especially one not attuned to personal feelings connected with separation and loss. It is hard to establish when such feelings result from separation anxiety and not some other anxiety. To make these determinations the interventionist must have adequate knowledge of the individual's prior history of separations and losses. The simplest, though not most accurate, indicator is the presence of signals that can be construed as implying future separation.

At the group and organizational levels historical patterns established for coping with one type of separation may exert a strong influence on how different types of separations are managed. This can make consequences of coping with anxiety even more likely to be dysfunctional. For example, if a group experienced positive results by engaging in denial, then it is probable that they will continue to prefer denial even when denial is the least productive coping mechanism available. Exploring the coping mechanisms used is a first step toward designing coping strategies that limit harmful outcomes and promote beneficial behavior.

As well as influencing the choice of coping behaviors, previous traumatic separations experienced by an organization may heighten its members' proclivity to interpret nonthreatening information as signals of real danger. This implies that groups prone to separation anxiety have greater difficulty in contending with change. For example, they may have significant and potentially debilitating separation anxiety as a response to technological and managerial innovations. In such groups it may be necessary to deal with the sources of previous separation anxiety before attempting new change. In general, when designing interventions for organizations it is crucial that prior experiences be weighed.

Setting

Components of the setting which might influence the effects of separation anxiety include the size of the organization, average job stress, organizational culture (e.g., bureaucratic, impersonal, paternalistic, meritocratic), organizational environment (e.g., stability, competitiveness, level of interdependence), organizational relationship to its surrounding community, internal diversity, and societal culture. Each of these factors can exert an influence both on the level of stress and the degree to which individuals and groups have a general feeling of separateness and isolation in their lives. To the degree that they feel alone and apart, it is likely that they will experience stress from separation anxiety. For example, a high level of competitiveness in the industry may result in a high base level of separation anxiety. This could lead to larger negative emotional reactions and resistances to dramatic changes such as mergers and acquisitions. Comparatively, the more interconnected and interdependent groups, organizations, and environment are, the less likely there is to be dramatic effects of separation anxiety.

The setting can also exert an influence on the types of coping behaviors employed. For example, a high level of interdependence makes withdrawal and detachment difficult. Likewise, loosely connected, impersonal and bureaucratic organizations with tall hierarchies make projection a more viable alternative. In general, the setting can shape the likelihood and degree of separation anxiety as well as the types of coping behaviors used.

Multiple Levels

Separation anxiety is affected by the level of the anticipated separation. As well as the individual level, such as when one or more individuals leave a group, anxiety can be caused by groups leaving an organization or the demise of an entire organization in an industry. For example, the recent spate of bankruptcies and takeovers among United States' banks have created a general state of anxiety in that industry.

Separation anxiety is often stimulated when group departures from an organization are imminent. Such situations typically arise when budget constraints are imposed, profits or revenues decrease, organizational leadership changes, and when organizations are acquired or merge. Acting as a microcosm of the organization, groups exhibit dynamics that reflect those found in the organization or industry in which they exist. For example, organizations that have recently implemented an early retirement program may find that project teams are disregarding the input of older members, even if they are key employees. In addition, interactions in nonthreatened groups may mirror the dynamics occurring in groups that have separating and leaving members. This is consistent with parallel group process (Alderfer, 1986). For example, a group in which no one is separating may engage in anger and conflict in response to similar behavior occurring in groups with whom they interact.

In general, organizational dynamics stimulated by separation anxiety are complex (cf. Krantz, 1985). In mergers and acquisitions, there is a further complicating factor: the other organization. Similar to what might happen in loosely connected organizations, a second organization fosters the projection of negative affect onto the other organization (Marks & Mirvis, 1985); blaming the other organization for their anxiety, uncertainty, and pain. This can have profound implications for managing postmerger integration.

Characteristics of the Separation

There are many characteristics of the separation that can influence separation anxiety. The communication(s) which stimulates separation anxiety can be direct or indirect. For example, a direct signal is one which explicitly states that someone or group will be leaving. Indirect cues more commonly accompany separations. For example, learning that the organization is facing budgetary constraints is an indirect cue of separation. With indirect cues who is leaving is ambiguous. In contrast, in this research members knew exactly who was leaving. When the separation cue is indirect, people respond by trying to clarify who is leaving. They may even begin to reshape boundaries to exclude existing members likely to leave or be asked to leave. Such groups may experience decreased communication and heightened internal competition as members attempt to secure their own positions in the group. When membership is homogenous and the signals are indirect it is more likely that people will respond like those in the All Leave condition: with denial and avoidance. Because of all the uncertainty surrounding indirect communications, it is often easier to manage anxiety when the communication is definite and direct. This requires early and clear communication about the consequences of bad news.

Direct and indirect communications can be accompanied by a safety signal (Seligman, 1975). A safety signal is a cue which indicates that an implied threat has become a real threat. The following excerpt from Seligman (1975) is a good example of the impact of a safety signal on separation anxiety:

When my wife and I began to leave our daughter with baby sitters during her first year, we noticed that Amy went from being placid to being increasingly fretful. We had adopted this strategy: when the baby sitter arrived for the first time, I introduced the baby sitter to Amy; then when they were engrossed in playing, my wife and I sneaked off. Our fading away, we hoped, would avoid the traumatic separation, with Amy wailing and protesting, that we knew would otherwise occur. It certainly seemed like the path of least resistance.

After we did this several times, we noticed Amy's increased anxiety. Kerry then objected to our strategy: "The safety-signal theory has definite predictions about sneaking off."

"How so?" I asked.

"When we leave Amy with no clear warning signal, that's just like an unpredictable shock," she said. "Amy is beginning to spend a lot of time in anxiety about separation, since she has learned that there is no predictor of leaving and therefore no predictor of our staying around. If, on the other hand, we go through an elaborate and explicit departure ritual, then Amy will learn that if the ritual hasn't occurred she doesn't have to worry."

This made a great deal of sense to me. . . . [We] have followed this ritual ever since. Soon thereafter, Amy went back to being placid. Incidentally, Amy at age five is a calm child, who does not seem at all worried about her parents leaving her. (pp. 151-52)

Some types of safety signals can be useful in all situations that have a potentially traumatic component. However, once they are abused, it is very likely that they will cease to function and will raise the overall level of anxiety. For example, in a corporate context if layoffs occur after losses mount even though upper management repeatedly indicates that there is no cause for alarm, employees will become increasingly anxious with each subsequent indication of loss, regardless of upper management's communications. Related to the existence of a safety signal is the anticipated time until separation is expected to occur. Anxiety and the use of protective coping mechanisms often increase exponentially as separation and change near. Organizations that do not prepare for this rapid change may find a sudden eruption of volcanic emotions shortly before separation.

Other characteristics of the separation include its anticipated permanence. For example, brief separations may stimulate less anxiety than permanent ones. This is an important issue to keep in mind when designing programs for gradual separation. Organizations in industries that have frequent separations might wish to compensate by having separation-reunion programs that are designed to acclimate employees with separation. Likewise, programs of short departures prior to an actual retirement may greatly facilitate executive succession.

Another factor is the degree of relationship modification. Small changes may have less of an impact than large ones (e.g., death, termination). If an organization has the luxury and is willing to be honest about its long term goals, it may be useful to start separation processes one small step at a time as opposed to a quick "clean cut." Indeed, handing out "pink slips" on

Friday afternoon is one of the most detrimental forms of termination for those staying in the organization. It may be useful, especially for those remaining in the organization, to incrementally shift reporting relationships and other structurally determined communication paths.

The expected degree of isolation following separation may also affect separation anxiety. Individuals and groups that have many attachments are less likely affected than those with few attachments. They have more opportunity to find social-emotional support and the separation makes up smaller portion of their total attachments. On the other hand, those with few attachments have great incentive to try to retain them. Organizations preparing for separation would be well advised to increase attachment behavior of its employees, including functional as well as social contact.

Perceptions of the fairness (cf. Lansberg, 1989) of the separation decision may also effect anxiety. For example, whether or not a group member was seen as deserving to be expelled from a group will determine how group members cope with the separation. It is more likely that projection of negative affect and characteristics onto the leaving member will occur if he or she is viewed as warranting exclusion. It is important that this tendency be held in check because short- and long-term consequences can include reduced communication during decision making, fear of being the next scapegoat, and guilty feelings. Perceptions of fairness are also shaped by factors already mentioned. For example, framing a separation as unfair is almost certainly necessary if group members are going to attempt to resist separation.

Finally, whether the separation is voluntary or involuntary may affect separation anxiety. It may be that voluntary separation is less stressful and has fewer detrimental long-term consequences than involuntary separation. This stress may decrease with the number of people who view the separation as voluntary. However, at some level determining whether a separation is voluntary or not is a philosophical question. Like perceptions of fairness, perceptions of voluntariness may be greatly mediated by factors mentioned above. Both perceptions of fairness and voluntariness may be highly determined by whether the individual and group perceive that they have made conscious choices and whether they are being disadvantaged by the separation. Even if the separation were viewed as fair and voluntary by all, it would still have an emotional effect.

Examples of the above five areas can be found in the research presented in this book. The simulation investigated how the number of leaving and staying members in a group (a specific characteristic of the anticipated separation) affects responses to separation anxiety during a simulated organizational merger (the setting in which separation anxiety occurred) at the individual and group levels. Historical separation experiences were not explored in depth. They were somewhat considered in the transitions distress questionnaire and in participant feedback. Only a few of the possible configurations of staying and leaving members were studied. As well as understanding the impact of each area independent of the others, future studies—especially field research—should examine other combinations, such as a large majority leaving the group while a small minority remains.

Method and Participants

Two other concerns needing attention in future research are the method used and the subjects studied. Aside from new simulations and other experiments which stimulate separation anxiety, future studies should examine separation anxiety and its effects in naturally occurring contexts. This would allow for an increased depth of data collected, with a richer view of the complexities of individual and group history, emotional effects, group dynamics, and the multiple effects of separation anxiety.

A general clinical method (cf. Berg & Smith, 1985) for studying separation anxiety could take three specific forms. One is an interview method used to examine people from various backgrounds and organizations. Long term in-depth interviewing should be employed to uncover data concerning the individual effects of separation anxiety over a wide range of situations. A second clinical method is to use group and individual interviews and questionnaires to examine specific organizations during the period beginning prior to and ending after separation. For example, companies should be studied longitudinally from the period before the announcement of a merger through era of operational integration. A third method, similar to the second, is action research. This entails making and studying interventions that are designed to cope more effectively with separation anxiety. For example, interventions can be implemented to help groups prepare for separation and readjust afterwards. This method allows for exploring separation as it occurs during the process of making useful interventions. One caveat of all research methods, and an especially tricky one with the clinical method, is that the interventionist's own separation anxiety will influence his or her behavior during the research enterprise and will, therefore, likely affect what is found during the research (cf. Berg, 1985).

There are many types of organizations and many classes of separations which could be studied. One which may be particularly well adapted to study is the military, especially the navy and coast guard. This is because military life involves routine and somewhat predictable separations from work groups (due to rotation, promotion, leaves), geographical locations, and family (during active sea duty especially). The continuous separating and attaching has likely led to well-established individual and institutional coping mechanisms that have likely gone unstudied. Organizations which offer outplacement services for terminated employees, and those which explicitly or implicitly guarantee lifetime employment, may be fruitful sites for clinical research. Other organizations which may also be well suited to study, as mentioned above, include hospitals, schools (all levels), performance arts groups, and governmental organizations which interact with or are composed of elected officials.

NONMANAGERIAL RELATIONSHIPS

Exploring nonmanagerial relationships can provide insight into effective management of separation anxiety in the work place. Many of the sources of anxiety and mediating factors found in organizations occur with greater intensity outside formal relationship structures. In addition, coping mechanisms may be easier to identify in social, family, and love relationships.

In this section, nonmanagerial relationships are examined using data collected from simulation participants. Several participants wrote about the effects of separation anxiety on nonmanagerial relationships. Their reports fall in three broad categories of coping strategies. These are anger and conflict, withdrawal and depression, and denial and avoidance (including intellectualization). All of these coping mechanisms are employed with the hope that they will help sever relationships before actual separation. However, they also add a new emotional dimension to the relationships, making the entire separation process more emotionally taxing. Dealing with separation anxiety through introspection, discussion, growth, and other methods of trying to understand and learn from current and past feelings and behaviors were not reported. Separation was generally discussed as an emotional and painful experience.

Anger and Conflict

The most common coping behaviors reported in the term papers appeared to be anger and fighting. While it may be perceived to help end a relationship, this reaction often has the side effect of increasing the attachment to a more intense emotional level. The comments of one student provide a rich example of coping via Anger and Conflict. This excerpt, previously seen in the Prelude, is repeated here and deciphered in greater detail. As is often the case with early self-reflection, the process starts with connecting current events. She clearly linked her classroom experience to her current interpersonal relations:

My description of how I had begun to behave with my boyfriend since I had accepted the idea that our separation next year was inevitable prompted other members of the class to talk about similar experiences. . . . We talked about our shared perceptions that the anger we often generated against individuals as a result of separation anxiety and in preparation for impending separation was easier to handle than the sadness we all felt would accompany a "civil" separation.

Increasing her level of introspection, she moved beyond her current relationships to consider the childhood roots of her responses to separation anxiety:

I had taken for granted my method of dealing with separation and did not yet realize that my behavior toward my boyfriend was part of a familiar pattern of dealing with separation anxiety that I had established in childhood. It had never occurred to me that people could end romantic relationships on a pleasant note. In my mind relationships of that nature only ended when turmoil existed to justify ending them. At that moment I was not aware of the fact that I had recently begun a process of creating a heightened level of tension in my relationships with many of my college friends, my parents, and especially my boyfriend in order to fulfill that requirement for severing relationships that existed in my mind.

The cycle of self-reflection continues as she considers the current pervasiveness of her separation anxiety experiences:

I realize now that separation anxiety was also carrying over into other aspects of my life—I had noticed a dramatic increase in my normal level of procrastination as well as the development of a very uncharacteristic pattern of non-decision making in my daily life. I had noticed these troubling developments but had stopped short of recognizing these behavioral patterns as reactions to the separations I would soon face as a graduating senior. I attributed my growing indecisiveness to other sources such as a wide array of options, lack of adequate information, and time constraints.

This self examination enabled her to deepen her awareness of the influences of her childhood experiences on her reactions to separation anxiety:

When I began to reflect upon the separations that I had experienced in my life and how they might affect my current perceptions, attitudes, and mechanisms for coping with separation, it became clear that my family life as a young child had a profound impact not only on my ability to separate but also my willingness to attach as well. Coping with separation from familiar people and places was a process that began early in life for me. My father worked for a government agency in my youth, and as a result, I had attended five different schools in different states and countries by the time I entered fifth grade. . . . I began to develop mechanisms of attaching and separating that I believed would minimize the pain I had felt upon my first separation from familiar people and surroundings.

When I think of the transition periods before and after each of our family's relocations, I recall anger, confusion, and an increasing dependence on members of my family for emotional support. In order to cope with the pain I associated with separation, I developed a pattern of becoming angry or upset with my childhood companions prior to my family's departure, of withdrawing from them and finally turning to my brother, sisters, and parents for social fulfillment and emotional support.

This excerpt eloquently explored coping with separation anxiety with anger and conflict and the connections between previous separations experiences and current coping behaviors, including her willingness to form attachments.

Another student considered separation anxiety as was stimulated during an all too common experience with roommate selection processes. He describes how his behavior changed from anger to withdrawal and how he finally began working towards a conscious resolution.

This year our group [of ten roommates] had the opportunity to get an eight-person room for next year. Two people had to leave the group of ten, and I was one of them. I'm still trying to understand why I agreed to leave. At the time it happened, I felt that I had been forced out by people who said that I was more "adaptable" to living with an alternative group. During the decision-making I felt very nervous, but after it was made, I was furious. I considered my former roommates selfish, uncaring, and undependable. I quit talking to them, sulked around for a few days, commenting to myself that "at least I know who my real friends are now." These bad feelings continued after the rooming lottery took place. . . . My first journal entry after the simulation class says, "I'm pissed about rooming (last night) still." The class was focused on intragroup dynamics. A little bit later I wrote, "I got crushed in some intragroup dynamics last night—it hurt. I want them to feel guilty" and then "Why don't I want to talk about my intragroup relations?"

. . . Suddenly I made the connection with my real life merger (rooming lottery) and wrote: "Is this because I'm not getting it and someone else is? Would I have felt this way in room draw if I had gotten in the octet?—Kind of excited?" Ding, ding, ding —bells started ringing. I decided that I had better try and find out why I had been so upset by room draw.

After extensive personal reflection, he came to realize that his roommates did not abandon him. They had expressed much concern and expended great effort to try and accommodate him. He then searched in greater depth for the origins of his feelings and behavior:

I realized that my uncharacteristic behavior was caused by a great fear of the pain associated with separation. Situations which threaten to leave me separated remind me of times in my life when I have been separated and have felt unimportant and unwanted. I can actually remember when I was three or four years old and my parents went on a trip and left me with one of my great aunts. I cried like crazy at first and felt abandoned. I can also remember that when my parents finally returned, I refused to go hug my mom and acted like I would rather stay with my aunt. It has just occurred to me that even at that young age, I was acting "irrationally" as I attempted to punish my mom for leaving me.

Several other participants wrote about a similar method for dealing with separation anxiety in relationships with parents and friends. It is interesting to note that in the majority of cases where anger was addressed, the individuals were separating from no more than two other people and the individual was leaving while the others were generally staying behind.

Withdrawal and Detachment

While some students reported anger before relationships ended and sadness afterwards, others detailed preseparation withdrawal and detachment. These cases generally concerned a single person separating from a larger group. One underclassman discussed his pattern of avoiding his graduating senior friends:

We never talk about the fact that our time remaining is short, but at the same time it is easy to notice that it is affecting our behavior. It is starting to affect me now. I don't go out of my way to see these people like I used to because I guess I'm trying to hide the facts to myself that I'm really going to miss these people. By slowly trying to remove myself from these friends, I am trying to avoid or make easier the inevitable good-bye. It has always been difficult for me to separate from close acquaintances. The night before I was to leave for college, my friends at home threw a big party for me. It was their way of saying good-bye. However, I didn't show up. I couldn't face the thought of not seeing these people for close to a year.

An underclasswoman shared a similar experience:

With my friends who are graduating this spring I began to distance myself about two weeks ago. I stopped calling them and spending time with them. I felt horrible about what I was doing but I believed that it was better in the long run. . . . Separation for me seems to be such an uncontrollable and final action. The manner in which I have chosen to deal with separation puts some control in my hands.

These two examples demonstrate how uncontrollable feelings associated with intense emotions cause actions designed to exert control. They also show how great the desire is to withdraw from situations in which the emotions are likely to "get out of hand."

An athlete discussed similar detachment feelings and some latent hostility when he was separated from his team due to injury:

Everyday I would attend practice, even hurt, but preparation for the upcoming game was imperative, therefore no attention was focused on me. Most evenings the main topic of conversation was practice. I no longer wished to participate. The nights before games were very difficult because everybody else (my teammates) would be preparing mentally and resting for the game the next day, but I found it hard to even think about the game, I would usually drink to forget about it. When game day rolled around, everybody was on edge, excited, and nervous about the game, adrenalin pumping and last minute preparations being made, and there I was trying unsuccessfully to still feel a part of the thrill of playing. It is truly hard. There were times when I found myself cheering against my teammates so they just might feel as though they needed me to win. It was hard to get excited over winning because if we won, I could not feel the tremendous satisfaction that a great team effort gives. And at times it hurt having everyone congratulate my friends and just apologize to me.

The above excerpts illustrate how withdrawal and detachment are used to reduce the intensity of emotions and to exert control over emotions and over situations believed to be uncontrollable. The passages also show how other emotions, such as hostility are also present during separation.

Denial and Avoidance

Various forms of denial are also prevalent coping behaviors. In discussing his reaction to oncoming separation, one participant gave a good example of denial: "The belief that I will stay in touch with everyone that I want to next year relieves a lot of the pressure for me." Forms of denial seemed to run along a continuum from denial of emotional reactions in the presence of others to absolute denial that a separation would occur. In dealing with a particularly emotional circumstance, one individual displayed the denial of emotions by intellectualizing the impending separation. The excerpt also shows how intellectualization is employed to exert control over intense and potentially debilitating emotions.

The threat of losing my most prized attachment figure, my mother, left me initially in a state of shock. Retreating from my emotions of fear and anxiety, I switched from being a frightened little girl to an almost professional woman. Instead of admitting to the tears streaming down my flushed cheeks and a pulse rate faster than the beat of Phil Collins on the snare, I requested answers to a plethora of technical medical questions. Demands for information on the size of the lump found replaced possible reassurances of my love for her before she entered the operating room. I was not sure how to deal with my own feelings; I was not ready to touch her emotions. Clarifying the actual surgical processes and post-operative procedures then became the most pressing issue for me to deal with. Given that our time on the phone had to be short, I lucked out on not having to continue the farce of interviewing the patient, not relating to my mother.

This recollection appeared to have been too emotionally charged for this participant. She abruptly changed the tone of her paper to the third person. The following passage is presented as it was written and includes all original typographical errors. In the continuation of the above excerpt the writer was apparently engaging in the behaviors being analyzed:

The challenge against the maintenance of a bond arouses anxeity through the threat to the security once held within that close bond. At first, a rush of fear and angst flood the emotions. Not wanting to deal with those feelings, an individual will behave on a seemingly non-emotional level, what I have called here professional. Fleeing away from the admission to the strong attachment that has been built and that soon will be broken seems to deny that any attachment exists to be separated from. Withdrawal from the situation is indicative of fearful behavior (Bowlby, 1975). The anxiety stems from the unwillingness to cut communications and ties with the attachment figure. Because the attachment process is long and involved marking the bond as an important force in an individual's development. a "normal" [non-psychotic] person will not be able to maintain that shroud over the real issue of separation very long.

This paragraph seems to display her anxiety both in the detached nature in which a personal topic was being addressed and in the variety of typographical errors and awkward sentence constructions it contains.

    Another form of denial is when the anxiety and emotions are recognized at some level and the individual struggles with controlling the painful emotions. In the following passage, the writer tries to cope with separation anxiety by actively attempting to repress emotions. In the text below a participant discusses how difficult it was to repress his feelings, especially when his soon-to-be-parted girlfriend was not present:

Both of us were silent for a while, lost in similar visions of separation. When I spoke, I said, "Yes, you're right, our relationship won't continue past graduation." I then switched the subject; R didn't stop me. We talked about how much work we had left—so much work that it seemed I'd never get done.

    That evening R had dinner with friends so I didn't see her for several hours. It was a break with habit and it caused me to miss her. Suddenly the emotions I'd felt earlier in the day came flooding back. I clammed up during dinner and hurried back to my room, I played some soothing music and tried to do some work, with little success. I waited for R until she returned and even then it was difficult for me not to miss her, even when I hugged her I had visions of our separation.

    Since then we have hardly talked about our inevitable separation. Occasionally R has tried to bring up the topic again, but each time I say that I don't have time to think about what life will be like after graduation; I have to concentrate on graduating. I have no idea, nor do I want to have one, of what I'm going to do over the summer or during next year. It's as if by not planning, by not thinking about it, it won't happen.

The intensity of emotions often has the effect of causing planning for the future to stop. This can be dangerous for the individual and the people who are dependent on him or her.

    Coping with separation anxiety through denial and repression often leads to a painful, but brief shock before separation. This is seen in the following excerpt in which one individual discusses the consequences of his denial of his and his girlfriend's imminent separation:

If the topic came up of separation we both agreed to worry about it later. We both knew that the day was arriving soon when we would be away from each other again, but we tried to pretend that it wasn't. Then when the day did come when we had to say good-bye, it was extremely difficult. It felt like a sudden thing and that we didn't know it was coming.

In recounting the nearing separation of a group to which he belonged another person explained, "We were trying to suppress the feeling of estrangement from emerging by searching for a common bond that would keep us together." In the majority of cases of reported denial, individuals perceived everyone in the relationship as leaving and no one was remaining or left behind.

In summary, these experiences illustrate how the findings from the simulation operate in real-life situations. The emotions felt were intense. The reported behavioral responses to separation anxiety were experienced only around transitions. While the reactions to separation anxiety appeared to be more complex and emotionally intense, the methods for dealing with separation anxiety were similar to those exhibited during the simulation: withdrawal and detachment, anger and fighting, and various degrees of denial. Withdrawal, accompanied by increased sadness, was reported as prevalent when an individual was leaving someone or some group. Anger and fighting were the dominant responses when the number of people leaving and staying was fairly equal. Denial was the principal reaction when all parties were perceived as leaving.

INTERGROUP RELATIONS IN GENERAL

Separation anxiety may also occur when people are not leaving others. It occurs in intergroup relations because individuals feel that they are separated as a result of their group memberships. For example, when Whites interact with Blacks feelings of being different and of belonging to separate groups foster separation anxiety. Other examples of intergroup events in organizations include project teams where cross-departmental, cross-hierarchical, or cross-functional interactions occur. In such situations, people often seek to amplify their differences in order to affirm membership and feel included in their existing groups. They may also attempt to hide or deny their differences in an attempt to avoid feeling excluded. Both behaviors have implications for the effectiveness of working together and understanding one another.

The intergroup effects of separation anxiety are often seen most clearly in interracial interactions (cf. Herbert, 1989; Thomas, 1986). Several individuals wrote about how being a racial minority often led them to feel a continuous state of high separation anxiety. One participant provided the following insightful passage. He first described his reactions to an event during a debriefing session:

In class, I found myself becoming very nervous while listening to T tell a story. T is from the South and she was talking about some of the racial problems that existed in her high school. Tears rolled down her face as she described both the physical and verbal abuse that white students heaped upon the Blacks. Although she completely disagreed with the actions of her white classmates, she did not do anything about it. She was afraid that making a comment to her white classmates, who were also her friends, would alienate her from them.

This situation caused him to reflect on a recent incident in his life which caused him to feel acutely separate. In it he describes many of the feelings and coping behaviors mentioned above, including denial, anger, and withdrawal.

Her story reminded me of a racial incident that happened to me last summer. I was in my car looking for the condominium garage door clicker to open the door and park my car, but I could not find it. Suddenly, a woman in a Jaguar passed by me and opened the door, so I decided to pull in behind her. She saw that I intended on entering the garage and attempted to physically obstruct me from entering the garage by leaving her car at the edge of the door so that there was no room for me to pull in. I then found my garage door opener (one that is possessed only by those who own a spot in the garage) and held it out the window so that she could see it, but she still did not move. I left my car and approached her. When I did this, she closed all her windows, locked her doors, and frantically waved me away. I turned and returned to my car, opened the door with the clicker, and then entered the garage (she had moved her car into her parking spot on the other side of the garage).

　　During this entire incident, I was frustrated and infuriated. At first, I rationalized that she was obstructing my entrance because all of the garage spaces are assigned and since I had not opened the door, she presumed that I did not own a space; this illogical thinking was quickly disregarded as other emotions began to surface. I was frustrated. I could not believe that she would not move. I was holding evidence in my hand proving my residency (although I am sure that if I was white, that I would not have to prove it) and she was not responding. When I exited my car to approach her, I was angry. What angered me the most, was that even after I proved to her that she was wrong, she would not even acknowledge her mistake or speak to me. When she locked her car doors and rolled up her windows, she made me feel as though I was some irrational beast, one that could not be communicated with. No person has the right to make another feel that way, but nonetheless, I did nothing about it. I allowed myself to be degraded and only turned my back and walked away from the situation. I allowed her to do *that* to <u>me</u>.

　　All I can remember from that incident is the thought, "control yourself, don't do anything that is going to embarrass mom or dad, or <u>yourself</u>." I felt helpless, I wanted so much to explode, but a stronger force was urging me to gain my composure and walk away from it all.

He continued delving deeper into the societal and personal roots for his reactions. In the following excerpt he shares a powerful story of daily coping with separation. It includes his feelings and behavior, and his interactions with those seeking to exclude him and those trying to help him feel included.

My behavioral reaction to the situation and that thought that kept echoing throughout my head during the entire episode were responses to my individual development as an outsider growing up in the in-group.

I was adopted at age two into a white household. I was an outsider both within my community and within my family. As we discussed in class, when you are associated with a group, but are different than all the other members of the group (especially with such a blatant characteristic as race), the member who is different often feels helpless, nervous, out of place, and frequently suffers from separation anxiety because he is the easiest person to cut off from the group. As a Black man in a white society, I encountered feelings of being in the out-group each and every day.

One example where I was clearly faced with the realization that I was Black, they were white, and everybody knew it, occurred one Sunday morning back in elementary school.

I remember an incident that occurred in church on several Sundays. The incident occurred during communion, as I was heading back to my seat, an older woman would lean over towards me and say "you nigger." This did not happen every Sunday, but it did happen frequently. I was embarrassed, startled, and scared when she said this to me. I continued to walk to my seat. I could not understand why someone would show such hatred towards me even though they did not know me. (This incident really scared me, and it only caused me to hate being black even more. My race continued to be nothing but a burden.) Time and time again, I encountered this woman and did nothing and said nothing. I never said anything to my family about this incident. (I hated being black because it made me separate from everyone else, and although I knew that others saw me as black, I placed the burden on myself to handle any racial problems that emerged so that others would not have to think about me being black.)

One Sunday morning, my brother happened to be right behind me when the woman leaned over and called me a "nigger." After services, while sitting at the breakfast table of my house, my brother asked me what that woman had said to me. I was extremely nervous when he asked me because discussing the issue would only exacerbate the differences that I was hoping to submerge. I did not want to feel as though I was an outsider even within my own family. My emotional response to the question and attempted denial of my blackness were so strong that I could not bring myself to say that she called me a nigger. Although the word nigger never came from my mouth, when I indicated that she had made a racial slur, they quickly figured out what she had said. My father immediately said that he wanted me to point her out to him next week so that he could speak to her. My mother told me that there were a lot of people out there who might say derogatory things to me, but I had to realize that they were ignorant, at least of race, and that I would have to ignore their racial stupidity. I also experienced one of the oddest sensations (this big lump formed in my throat and I was unable to speak) when my brothers interrupted my mother and promised that, next week, I could stand between them during communion and that they would punch the woman if she said anything to me. It made me feel secure knowing that I had them there to help/protect me.

My feelings of security were ended abruptly when the discussion of race continued, and my brother decided to share an educational story with the family. He was in high school at the time, and was saying how someone had once referred to a black classmate as a *nigger*. (The black student was not present at the time.) Even though that upset him and he said something to that person, he told me that some people might call me a *nigger* and that I should only disregard what they say because it is out of ignorance. I hated hearing the word *nigger*, but it hurt me even more coming from my brother's lips. It was as though my entire facade had been destroyed—they all saw me as a black person and an outsider, and there was nothing I could do.

The above example is rich with information. It displays the full range of intense emotions and behaviors. It also illustrates how attempts to include someone can serve to unintentionally emphasize difference and increase feelings of separation. It is especially painful given that the feelings of separateness took place in a close, open, and highly attached family.

Racially stimulated separation anxiety was also discussed by a White man during an interview. A religious person, he described his conflicts around searching for a church in which he could feel comfortable. After having investigated all the local White churches, he grappled with the idea of attending services at a Black church. He said that he felt like he was separating himself from his own race, and felt very separate from the Blacks in the church he attended. Yet, he said that at a religious level he felt far more comfortable there than he did at any of the White churches he had attended in the past. After some time at the Black church, he indicated that he had begun to deal with his feelings of separation and could more easily embrace other members of the congregation.

In general, separation anxiety complicates intergroup interactions. Differences between people represented by an intergroup boundary foster separation anxiety at two levels: being separate from the different group and the possibility of being separate from one's own group. Becoming separate from one's own group is rarely acknowledged as a source of anxiety. Recognizing this and other sources of separation anxiety is important when trying to devise conscious and explicit coping strategies.

Intragroup boundaries often coincide with boundaries caused by separation decisions. The boundary along which groups are separated is frequently aligned with identity group (e.g., Black-White and male-female boundaries) or other pre-existing boundaries (e.g., departmental boundaries). For example, when lay-offs occur it is currently not at all unusual that the majority of those forced to leave belong to one identity or organizational group. During periods of heightened separation anxiety, intragroup boundaries may strengthen as members turn to one another for support and feelings of inclusion and cast negative projections onto dissimilar group members whom they seek to exclude.

MANAGERIAL RELATIONSHIPS

Three fundamental questions should be addressed when applying the theory and research to managerial situations. What are the characteristics of the organization that influence separation anxiety? How might anxiety be detected? What might be included in programs designed to deal with anxiety produced during mergers, acquisitions, and change in general? These questions are addressed here to help professionals think about how to apply the theory and research presented in this book in managerial settings.

Organizational Types

Organizations have structures, personnel, and tasks and operate in industries that influence the intensity of separation anxiety. Structural characteristics can have a large impact on the severity of and reactions to separation anxiety. For example, very tall hierarchies and very large organizations may foster separation anxiety because of the lack of contact between employee groups. This may help explain why organizations that are prone to separation anxiety because they are in rapidly changing industries function well with strict limits on plant size (e.g., Gore Associates).

There are basically two types of organizations that can expect to have intense employee reactions to separation. One is where the base level of separation anxiety is expected to be high because of the nature of the work, work relationships, customer relationships, employee diversity, and nature of the industry. Generally, these are organizations where attachments to the organization are weak, a substantial portion of relationships are short term, or the environment is particularly fluid or hostile. In these organizations, the base level of anxiety can exponentially amplify anxiety coming from discrete change processes. Employees may even find the planned change a useful object on which to project negative emotions already in existence. In such cases we can expect to find the change resisted strongly.

Managers in such organizations would be wise to become sensitive to how the usual level of separation anxiety is coped with. This is critically important before dramatic changes are implemented. Informally created coping mechanisms should be identified and worked with when undertaking large transitions. Coping mechanisms that have been unconsciously developed for dealing with recurrent anxiety will likely exert themselves with great force as anxiety increases. For example, a scapegoat group may find itself the victim of increasingly violent harassment during organizational change. To ameliorate the negative effects of anxiety, new outlets for anxiety stimulated by large change can be helpful. It may also be important to build employee attachments to other parts of the organization through increased contact and work interdependence. When relationships are being modified new and stable relationships can provide an anchor and source of continuity. One potential caveat of this strategy is that people who purposely join this type of organization in order to avoid making strong attachments will need special attention when nurturing new attachments and may require some psychological-developmental work.

A similar strategy is to form transitional attachments (cf. Winnicott, 1953). These can be new and temporary relationships formed as a bridge from one set of relationships to the next. However, they pose the potential problem of needing to separate from an additional set of relationships to accommodate change.

The second type of organization that can expect particularly intense reactions to separation is one in which the base level of separation anxiety is very low and there are a small number of very strong attachments. Most notable among these are family-owned or controlled firms, firms with charismatic leadership, and those that assure lifetime employment. In these organizations, employees generally feel safe and secure as long as the object of attachment, be it a person or an unwritten promise, remains intact. Employees may join these organizations because of an intense desire to maintain strong stable attachments. When the attachment is called into question, frenzied reactions may occur as a primary source of stability loses reliability. This can occur, for example, when a charismatic CEO announces his or her retirement.

It is common for people in these organizations to sabotage separation. For example, incompetent replacements may be chosen in order to provide an excuse for key people to remain. Similarly, productivity may wane, communication may become strained or stop altogether, and interpersonal problems may rise. Decision making can become labored if employees feel that successful work might aid separation.

The problems posed by this type of organization, where attachments are few and quite strong, may be counteracted in a manner similar to that useful for organizations where there is a high base level of separation anxiety. Attachments to others need to be formed to provide continuity and ease separation. A weaning process that includes repeated temporary separations may also be useful. In entrepreneurial preprofessional management organizations, transitions can sometimes be aided by professionalizing the firm. However, managers should be careful not to instigate too many changes in this direction before employees are able to accept the transformation.

Detecting Anxiety

The detection of anxiety is vital for it requires the manager to be acutely aware of employee emotions and behaviors. It is important to remember that both staying and leaving members share anxiety. In order to effectively manage their anxiety, it must first be detected. In general, any marked change in emotions or behavior can signal the presence of increased anxiety. While some managers have remarkable intuition, it generally takes extensive training and personal reflection to accurately identify general anxiety, much less separation anxiety. It is especially difficult to detect because behaviors that indicate anxiety are often a source of comfort to managers. For example, management must be sensitive to the temptation to allow employees to project negative attributes and emotions onto leaving members. Projection onto others can leave managers feeling safe and filled with self-assured thoughts such as "Thank goodness they're not picking on me!" It can also result in bad decision making and unproductive work. Managers should also be careful to resist the temptation to view complaints about separation as indications that people are unwilling to cope. It may be that they are simply asking for support and comfort during a painful transition. An angry managerial response, such as, "Stop complaining and get on with the work!" would likely increase needs for support by further aggravating employees who feel they are working harder than ever to cope with changed responsibilities, new relationships, and the emotional aftermath of separation.

Leaving members being played off one another and not allowed to unite are another indication of systemic anxiety. This is also a behavior pattern which managers may find tolerable because of the lack of personal emotional consequences. It is generally behavior that does not have positive functional consequences. Indeed, it can increase feelings of anger, depression, and guilt as people feel badly about using others and feel angry and depressed at being used.

Denial is an especially seductive coping mechanism that managers find difficult to detect. This is especially true when denial takes the form of the belief that extra-hard work will stall separation and reverse separation decisions. It is also a coping mechanism that can have negative long-term consequences if employees feel they have been misled or deceived. Likewise, it can lead to a dramatic shock when separation does occur.

Another consequence of anxiety is that it causes perceived helplessness which leads to unproductive work. When these feelings are displayed by poor performers they can easily be misinterpreted. In such cases poor performers are likely to be a target of negative projection. In general, feelings of depression and helplessness often herald splitting and projection. In contrast to perceived helplessness, exerting control is another indication of anxiety and of being emotionally overwhelmed. For example, someone who is hyper-vigilant or acting in a "petty bureaucrat" manner may be responding to increased anxiety about relationships by displaying their certainty of, and desire to protect, rules and procedures. When anxiety causes strict rule adherence, the behavior of rigid and inflexible employees is often misinterpreted.

Managers not familiar with the effects of separation anxiety may act in ways that foster denial, projection, and detachment because of a desire to avoid anger and conflict. The findings from this research show that in some situations avoiding anger and conflict is tantamount to obstructing good task work. Managers wishing to accurately detect separation anxiety may attempt to use their own feelings as a barometer. However, this requires a high degree of emotional self-awareness on the part of the manager.

Managing Employee Anxiety

Developing programs to manage anxiety is a complex process because emotions and anxiety can be intense and can fluctuate rapidly. A high level of expertise is required. Several ideas are already being used to cope with transitions, though not specifically with separation anxiety. These include rituals, team building focused on transitions, individual counseling, outplacement, and other postseparation programs.

While preparing for change is less frequent, enlightened organizations are already dealing with the consequences of separation anxiety on mergers and acquisitions. Many organizations have successful outplacement programs and other systems for coping with mergers and acquisitions and other sources of separation. Some of these include dealing with separation in an explicit way. For example, by keeping employees informed and including them in decision making, by formally allowing for opportunities for discussion of anticipated consequences, by active and participatory planning for evolving roles and future relationships, and by being generally attentive to the real psychological consequences of separation.

Implementing similar programs can have beneficial effects. However, experts should serve as advisors to such projects because of the high level of training required to be able to identify sources of anxiety and appropriate responses. Some of the systems can actually have a deleterious effect if they are not part of a carefully developed and rigorously monitored overall plan. For example, one organization that had an active outplacement department kept remaining and leaving employees separate. In this company added anxiety was created because workers remaining in the organization saw, but were discouraged from interacting with, those leaving. A common display of anxiety was witnessed every time the elevator passed the floor that housed the outplacement department. Employees were frequently heard to exclaim, "Please don't stop on the tenth floor!"

Rituals may help ease the impact of negative emotions. They allow for the relatively safe expression of emotion. They also mark transition points and can act as safety signals. However, they generally do not help the learning process, do not help avoid future anxiety, and do not prepare either those leaving or those remaining for their future relationships. Along with ritual events are the important uses of symbols of change. It has already been indicated that symbols can have an anxiety-producing effect when they are construed as implying future separation. Symbols can also have a reassuring influence (Boulian, 1974).

Much information indicates that feelings change rapidly over the course of a separation. To be responsive to this, programs should have a self-monitoring capacity that increases the responsiveness of the program to quick changes in employee attitudes. For example, we have seen that those who anticipate being isolated tend to quickly withdraw from interaction.

The tendency to withdraw from relationships, once recognized, may be counteracted by programs that deal with those fears and act in ways to reduce isolation. This can potentially occur by helping those leaving form new attachments and by helping those remaining and leaving to develop expectations for modified relationships following separation. Caution should be taken not to view isolation as a problem which is solely felt by those leaving. In the short run that would only serve to exacerbate feelings of isolation.

Another tendency to be monitored and considered when designing anxiety management programs is exerting control when anxiety becomes intense. Programs can be designed to take advantage of this tendency and direct this energy toward productive ends. For example, directly involving employees in the implementation of change planning processes can reduce feelings of not being in control. That people often want to exert control, unify, and generally work harder when anxiety rises suggests that separation information should be announced in a timely fashion. One caveat is that other factors may cause such information to have the opposite effect of promoting withdrawal and detachment. A second caution is that if there are no mutually accepted activities into which the energy stimulated by anxiety can be directed, the anxiety may result in pernicious behavior. A third caveat is that providing such information must not be abused because false or deceptive communication may also stimulate anxiety. It is not a good long term strategy to raise anxiety for the sole purpose of increasing productivity. It leads to resentment, employee burn-out, and sabotage.

As with any program used to manage anxiety, it is worthwhile to help employees explore all sources of separation anxiety. This enables people to understand what part of the anxiety is due to upcoming separation, what part comes from pre-existing conditions (e.g., diversity of employees) and what part is generated by prior separation experiences. If the sources of emotional changes are correctly attributed, there is less likelihood that communications will be misinterpreted and discounted. Sorting through the sources of separation anxiety can also be a powerful educational experience with benefits for all future relationship changes.

Acknowledging separations can also enable discussion of anticipated and preferred behavior following separation. Until separations are acknowledged, the idea that relationships are usually not completely terminated but are modified cannot be examined. Active relationship modification through the discussion of future roles, feelings, and behavior can establish continuity that helps limit the disturbing effects of separation anxiety while allowing the beneficial consequences of separation to emerge.

SUMMARY

In summary, anxiety management programs should have three components. They need to have a monitoring function so that they can both identify anxiety and respond to changing emotions and behavior. They should have a component to deal with the emotions raised. For example, ritualized events, symbols of change, and individual and team counseling can ease and redirect intense emotions. Finally, they need to consider the planning and development of relationship changes including new attachments and separations. For example, shared decision making, forming transitional attachments for the sake of continuity, and repeated temporary separations can all help the planning and implementation of relationship change.

Managers should remember that anxiety and emotions do not have to be colorfully displayed to be having a profound effect and that both those staying and leaving have anxiety. Programs should be designed to deal with both parties of a separation. Both sides also have the potential to be disrupted by separation and both have the capacity to benefit emotionally, psychologically, and professionally.

For mergers and acquisitions in particular, this work implies that many behaviors witnessed prior to actual merger or acquisition are influenced strongly by dynamics rooted in separation anxiety. Organizational managers would benefit from becoming sensitive to separation anxiety. Managing both the fears of separation and separations that actually occur is of crucial importance to successful large-scale change.

Appendix 1:
Previous Transitions Questionnaire

Name: _____

Age: ____

Gender: ___Male ___Female

Race: ___White ___Black ___Hispanic ___Asian

___Native American Other (specify) _____

Religious Heritage (religion at birth):

___Catholic ___Jewish ___Muslim ___Hindu

___Buddhist ___Protestant _____
(specify denomination)

Other (specify)_____

Converted religion as an adult: ___Yes ___No

In the left-hand Blank beside each transition below, please indicate the number of times you have had each transition and the date of the latest one. Whether or not you have experienced them, on the scale underneath each question please circle the number which corresponds to how emotionally stressful each category of transition is for you. Stress refers to the immediate and lasting effects of a category of transition. When judging the stress of past transitions, be sure to also reflect upon seemingly unassociated events that occured shortly before, during and shortly after the transition. Note: Family of origin refers to the family you were born into, family of creation refers to the family that you create.

Example

Number of Transitions	Date of Most Recent Transition (Year)			

| 1 | 1985 | Marriage(s). | | |

0	1	2	3	4
Question Does Not Apply	Very Stressful	Somewhat Stressful	Slightly Stressful	Not at All Stressful

---

Number of Transitions | Date of Most Recent Transition (Year)

_____ _____   Move(s) of residence location of family of origin.

0	1	2	3	4
Question does Not Apply	Very Stressful	Somewhat Stressful	Slightly Stressful	Not at All Stressful

_____ _____   School change(s) (include all changes, e.g. elementary to high school = 1 and from one high school to a different high school also = 1).

0	1	2	3	4
Question does Not Apply	Very Stressful	Somewhat Stressful	Slightly Stressful	Not at All Stressful

_____   _____   Departed home of family of origin for school (e.g. boarding school, college, graduate school).

0	1	2	3	4
Question does Not Apply	Very Stressful	Somewhat Stressful	Slightly Stressful	Not at All Stressful

_____   _____   Departed home of family of origin for work, to start a family of your own, or to become independent.

0	1	2	3	4
Question does Not Apply	Very Stressful	Somewhat Stressful	Slightly Stressful	Not at All Stressful

_____   _____   Parental Divorce(s)/Separation(s).

0	1	2	3	4
Question does Not Apply	Very Stressful	Somewhat Stressful	Slightly Stressful	Not at All Stressful

_____   _____   Death of parent(s).

0	1	2	3	4
Question does Not Apply	Very Stressful	Somewhat Stressful	Slightly Stressful	Not at All Stressful

_____   _____   Birth(s)/Adoption(s) of sibling.

0	1	2	3	4
Question does Not Apply	Very Stressful	Somewhat Stressful	Slightly Stressful	Not at All Stressful

_____   _____   Death of sibling(s).

0	1	2	3	4
Question does Not Apply	Very Stressful	Somewhat Stressful	Slightly Stressful	Not at All Stressful

_____   _____   Death of close friend(s).

0	1	2	3	4
Question does Not Apply	Very Stressful	Somewhat Stressful	Slightly Stressful	Not at All Stressful

_____   _____   Death of spouse(s).

0	1	2	3	4
Question does Not Apply	Very Stressful	Somewhat Stressful	Slightly Stressful	Not at All Stressful

_____   _____   Death of child(ren).

0	1	2	3	4
Question does Not Apply	Very Stressful	Somewhat Stressful	Slightly Stressful	Not at All Stressful

_____   _____   Marriage(s).

0	1	2	3	4
Question does Not Apply	Very Stressful	Somewhat Stressful	Slightly Stressful	Not at All Stressful

_____   _____   Divorce(s)/Separation(s).

0	1	2	3	4
Question does Not Apply	Very Stressful	Somewhat Stressful	Slightly Stressful	Not at All Stressful

_____   _____   Job change(s) (include all changes which required
you to work with a new group of people on a regular
basis. Do not include jobs while a full-time student
or during summer vacations or change from full-time
student to post school career).

0	1	2	3	4
Question does Not Apply	Very Stressful	Somewhat Stressful	Slightly Stressful	Not at All Stressful

_____   _____   Career change(s) (e.g. peace corps to banking,
employed to pensioner. Do not include jobs while a
full-time student or during summer vacations or
change from full-time student to post-school career).

0	1	2	3	4
Question does Not Apply	Very Stressful	Somewhat Stressful	Slightly Stressful	Not at All Stressful

_____ _____ Birth(s)/Adoption(s) in family of creation.

0	1	2	3	4
Question does Not Apply	Very Stressful	Somewhat Stressful	Slightly Stressful	Not at All Stressful

_____ _____ Move(s) of residence location of family of creation (include all moves after your last move away from your parents).

0	1	2	3	4
Question does Not Apply	Very Stressful	Somewhat Stressful	Slightly Stressful	Not at All Stressful

_____ _____ Child(ren) departed for school (e.g. boarding school, college, graduate school).

0	1	2	3	4
Question does Not Apply	Very Stressful	Somewhat Stressful	Slightly Stressful	Not at All Stressful

_____ _____ Child(ren) departed home for work, to start a family of their own, or to become independent.

0	1	2	3	4
Question does Not Apply	Very Stressful	Somewhat Stressful	Slightly Stressful	Not at All Stressful

_____ _____ Marriage(s) of child(ren).

0	1	2	3	4
Question does Not Apply	Very Stressful	Somewhat Stressful	Slightly Stressful	Not at All Stressful

Number of transitions that you have experienced which you would characterize as being at least slightly traumatic. _____

Appendix 2: Merger and Acquisition Simulation Questionnaire

You are about to participate in a merger and acquisition simulation. Part of the exercise will involve forming groups that will work on a specific task. More information will be handed out after everyone completes this questionnaire.

There are about 30 questions below. You have five minutes to complete this questionnaire.

BIOGRAPHICAL DATA SECTION

Name _____

___ Male   ___ Female
___ White   ___ Black   ___ People of Color

Approximate number of close personal relationships in your life.   ___

Approximate number of people whom you can count on for support during a crisis.   ___

Size of family of origin (i.e. you, your parents and siblings).   ___

SIMULATION QUESTIONS SECTION

Please circle the response which best characterizes your reaction to the following statements.

The quality of my group's work will be the best compared to all others.

1	2	3	4	5	6
Agree	Agree Somewhat	Agree Slightly	Disagree Slightly	Disagree Somewhat	Disagree

I will like my group a great deal.

1	2	3	4	5	6
Agree	Agree Somewhat	Agree Slightly	Disagree Slightly	Disagree Somewhat	Disagree

I will make a large contribution to my group's work.

1	2	3	4	5	6
Agree	Agree Somewhat	Agree Slightly	Disagree Slightly	Disagree Somewhat	Disagree

The group will enhance my ability to work.

1	2	3	4	5	6
Agree	Agree Somewhat	Agree Slightly	Disagree Slightly	Disagree Somewhat	Disagree

The group will detract from my ability to work.

1	2	3	4	5	6
Agree	Agree Somewhat	Agree Slightly	Disagree Slightly	Disagree Somewhat	Disagree

I will have a great sense of "feeling included" in my group.

1	2	3	4	5	6
Agree	Agree Somewhat	Agree Slightly	Disagree Slightly	Disagree Somewhat	Disagree

I will be understood by my group's members.

1	2	3	4	5	6
Agree	Agree Somewhat	Agree Slightly	Disagree Slightly	Disagree Somewhat	Disagree

I will understand my group's members.

1	2	3	4	5	6
Agree	Agree Somewhat	Agree Slightly	Disagree Slightly	Disagree Somewhat	Disagree

My group's members will be open to my suggestions.

1	2	3	4	5	6
Agree	Agree Somewhat	Agree Slightly	Disagree Slightly	Disagree Somewhat	Disagree

I will be open to the suggestions of my group's members.

1	2	3	4	5	6
Agree	Agree Somewhat	Agree Slightly	Disagree Slightly	Disagree Somewhat	Disagree

I will feel left out of my group.

1	2	3	4	5	6
Agree	Agree Somewhat	Agree Slightly	Disagree Slightly	Disagree Somewhat	Disagree

Current Emotion Section

Below you will find descriptive words that refer to emotions. Please circle the number which best represents your current emotional state.

Afraid	1 Very	2 Somewhat	3 Slightly	4 A Little	5 Not at All
Content	1 Very	2 Somewhat	3 Slightly	4 A Little	5 Not at All
Safe	1 Very	2 Somewhat	3 Slightly	4 A Little	5 Not at All

Depressed	1 Very	2 Somewhat	3 Slightly	4 A Little	5 Not at All
Secure	1 Very	2 Somewhat	3 Slightly	4 A Little	5 Not at All
On Edge	1 Very	2 Somewhat	3 Slightly	4 A Little	5 Not at All
Angry	1 Very	2 Somewhat	3 Slightly	4 A Little	5 Not at All
Anxious	1 Very	2 Somewhat	3 Slightly	4 A Little	5 Not at All
Lonely	1 Very	2 Somewhat	3 Slightly	4 A Little	5 Not at All
Happy	1 Very	2 Somewhat	3 Slightly	4 A Little	5 Not at All
Sad	1 Very	2 Somewhat	3 Slightly	4 A Little	5 Not at All
Pleased	1 Very	2 Somewhat	3 Slightly	4 A Little	5 Not at All
Sure of Self	1 Very	2 Somewhat	3 Slightly	4 A Little	5 Not at All
Carefree	1 Very	2 Somewhat	3 Slightly	4 A Little	5 Not at All
Calm	1 Very	2 Somewhat	3 Slightly	4 A Little	5 Not at All
Comfortable	1 Very	2 Somewhat	3 Slightly	4 A Little	5 Not at All
Tense	1 Very	2 Somewhat	3 Slightly	4 A Little	5 Not at All
Confident	1 Very	2 Somewhat	3 Slightly	4 A Little	5 Not at All

Jittery	1	2	3	4	5
	Very	Somewhat	Slightly	A Little	Not at All

Nervous	1	2	3	4	5
	Very	Somewhat	Slightly	A Little	Not at All

Appendix 3: Merger and Acquisition Simulation Questionnaire #5

You have five minutes to complete this questionnaire.

Name _____

SIMULATION QUESTIONS SECTION

Please circle the response which best characterizes your reaction to the following statements.

The quality of my group's work was the best compared to all others.

1	2	3	4	5	6
Agree	Agree Somewhat	Agree Slightly	Disagree Slightly	Disagree Somewhat	Disagree

I like my group a great deal.

1	2	3	4	5	6
Agree	Agree Somewhat	Agree Slightly	Disagree Slightly	Disagree Somewhat	Disagree

I made a large contribution to my group's work.

1	2	3	4	5	6
Agree	Agree Somewhat	Agree Slightly	Disagree Slightly	Disagree Somewhat	Disagree

I am happy with the superiors in our company (UCI).

1	2	3	4	5	6
Agree	Agree Somewhat	Agree Slightly	Disagree Slightly	Disagree Somewhat	Disagree

The group enhanced my ability to work.

1	2	3	4	5	6
Agree	Agree Somewhat	Agree Slightly	Disagree Slightly	Disagree Somewhat	Disagree

The group detracted from my ability to work.

1	2	3	4	5	6
Agree	Agree Somewhat	Agree Slightly	Disagree Slightly	Disagree Somewhat	Disagree

I had a great sense of "feeling included" in my group.

1	2	3	4	5	6
Agree	Agree Somewhat	Agree Slightly	Disagree Slightly	Disagree Somewhat	Disagree

My group chose the best questions from the list.

1	2	3	4	5	6
Agree	Agree Somewhat	Agree Slightly	Disagree Slightly	Disagree Somewhat	Disagree

I was understood by my group's members.

1	2	3	4	5	6
Agree	Agree Somewhat	Agree Slightly	Disagree Slightly	Disagree Somewhat	Disagree

I understood my group's members.

1	2	3	4	5	6
Agree	Agree Somewhat	Agree Slightly	Disagree Slightly	Disagree Somewhat	Disagree

My group's members were open to my suggestions.

1	2	3	4	5	6
Agree	Agree Somewhat	Agree Slightly	Disagree Slightly	Disagree Somewhat	Disagree

I was open to the suggestions of my group's members.

1	2	3	4	5	6
Agree	Agree Somewhat	Agree Slightly	Disagree Slightly	Disagree Somewhat	Disagree

I felt left out of my group.

1	2	3	4	5	6
Agree	Agree Somewhat	Agree Slightly	Disagree Slightly	Disagree Somewhat	Disagree

I was angry with my group.

1	2	3	4	5	6
Agree	Agree Somewhat	Agree Slightly	Disagree Slightly	Disagree Somewhat	Disagree

There was one member of our group who would probably be identified unanimously as our group's leader.

1	2	3	4	5	6
Agree	Agree Somewhat	Agree Slightly	Disagree Slightly	Disagree Somewhat	Disagree

I participated more than all the other group members.

1	2	3	4	5	6
Agree	Agree Somewhat	Agree Slightly	Disagree Slightly	Disagree Somewhat	Disagree

I had the feeling of being closer to my group members after the simulation ended than I did before it began.

1	2	3	4	5	6
Agree	Agree Somewhat	Agree Slightly	Disagree Slightly	Disagree Somewhat	Disagree

Without me, the group would have chosen some significantly different questions.

1	2	3	4	5	6
Agree	Agree Somewhat	Agree Slightly	Disagree Slightly	Disagree Somewhat	Disagree

I believe that one of the primary underlying issues that we were dealing with and that influenced our behavior was group separation.

1	2	3	4	5	6
Agree	Agree Somewhat	Agree Slightly	Disagree Slightly	Disagree Somewhat	Disagree

I believe that one of the primary underlying issues that we were dealing with and that influenced our behavior was individual separation.

1	2	3	4	5	6
Agree	Agree Somewhat	Agree Slightly	Disagree Slightly	Disagree Somewhat	Disagree

CURRENT EMOTION SECTION

Below you will find descriptive words that refer to emotions. Please circle the number which best represents your current emotional state.

Afraid	1 Very	2 Somewhat	3 Slightly	4 A Little	5 Not at All
Content	1 Very	2 Somewhat	3 Slightly	4 A Little	5 Not at All
Safe	1 Very	2 Somewhat	3 Slightly	4 A Little	5 Not at All
Depressed	1 Very	2 Somewhat	3 Slightly	4 A Little	5 Not at All
Secure	1 Very	2 Somewhat	3 Slightly	4 A Little	5 Not at All
On Edge	1 Very	2 Somewhat	3 Slightly	4 A Little	5 Not at All

Angry	1 Very	2 Somewhat	3 Slightly	4 A Little	5 Not at All
Anxious	1 Very	2 Somewhat	3 Slightly	4 A Little	5 Not at All
Lonely	1 Very	2 Somewhat	3 Slightly	4 A Little	5 Not at All
Happy	1 Very	2 Somewhat	3 Slightly	4 A Little	5 Not at All
Sad	1 Very	2 Somewhat	3 Slightly	4 A Little	5 Not at All
Pleased	1 Very	2 Somewhat	3 Slightly	4 A Little	5 Not at All
Sure of Self	1 Very	2 Somewhat	3 Slightly	4 A Little	5 Not at All
Carefree	1 Very	2 Somewhat	3 Slightly	4 A Little	5 Not at All
Calm	1 Very	2 Somewhat	3 Slightly	4 A Little	5 Not at All
Comfortable	1 Very	2 Somewhat	3 Slightly	4 A Little	5 Not at All
Tense	1 Very	2 Somewhat	3 Slightly	4 A Little	5 Not at All
Confident	1 Very	2 Somewhat	3 Slightly	4 A Little	5 Not at All
Jittery	1 Very	2 Somewhat	3 Slightly	4 A Little	5 Not at All
Nervous	1 Very	2 Somewhat	3 Slightly	4 A Little	5 Not at All

GROUP PROCESS QUESTIONS

Please circle the response which best characterizes your reaction to the following statements.

I had not a single strong alliance with any member of my group during the task discussion.

1	2	3	4	5	· 6
Agree	Agree Somewhat	Agree Slightly	Disagree Slightly	Disagree Somewhat	Disagree

There were two members of my group who were unfairly trying to influence the group for their own benefit.

1	2	3	4	5	6
Agree	Agree Somewhat	Agree Slightly	Disagree Slightly	Disagree Somewhat	Disagree

We chose one question to satisfy leaving group member(s).

1	2	3	4	5	6
Agree	Agree Somewhat	Agree Slightly	Disagree Slightly	Disagree Somewhat	Disagree

After we chose a question to satisfy leaving-group member(s), we concentrated on the more important work of the task.

1	2	3	4	5	6
Agree	Agree Somewhat	Agree Slightly	Disagree Slightly	Disagree Somewhat	Disagree

I teamed up with one group member in particular during the task discussion.

1	2	3	4	5	6
Agree	Agree Somewhat	Agree Slightly	Disagree Slightly	Disagree Somewhat	Disagree

The majority of the group did not want to discuss issues concerning leaving group member(s).

1	2	3	4	5	6
Agree	Agree Somewhat	Agree Slightly	Disagree Slightly	Disagree Somewhat	Disagree

I wanted to discuss issues concerning leaving group members far more than the rest of my group did.

1	2	3	4	5	6
Agree	Agree Somewhat	Agree Slightly	Disagree Slightly	Disagree Somewhat	Disagree

Bibliography

Alderfer, C.P. 1980. Consulting to Underbounded Systems. In C.P. Alderfer, and C.L. Cooper (Eds.), *Advances in Experiential Social Processes, Volume 2*, London: Wiley.

Alderfer, C.P. 1986. An Intergroup Perspective on Group Dynamics. In J. Lorsch (Ed.), *Handbook of Organizational Behavior*. Englewood Cliffs, New Jersey: Prentice-Hall.

Alderfer, C.P., C. Alderfer, L. Tucker, & R.C. Tucker. 1980. Diagnosing Race Relations in Management. *Journal of Applied Behavioral Science* 16: 135-166.

Alderfer, C.P., L.D. Brown, R.E. Kaplan, & K.K. Smith. 1984. *Group Relations and Organizational Diagnosis*. New York: Wiley.

Aronfreed, J. 1969. The Concept of Internalization. In D. Goslin (Ed.), *Handbook of Socialization Theory and Research*. Chicago: Rand McNally.

Astrachan, J.H. 1989. *Group and Individual Responses to Separation Anxiety Evoked by a Mergers and Acquisitions Simulation.* Doctoral Dissertation, Yale University: New Haven, Connecticut.

Astrachan, J.H. 1988. Group and Individual Responses to Separation Anxiety as Stimulated by Organizational Change: A Mergers and Acquisitions Simulation. *Organizational Behavior, Working Paper Series A*, no. 80. New Haven: Yale School of Organization and Management.

Axlerod, R., & W.D. Hamilton. 1981. The Evolution of Cooperation. *Science*, 211 (27): 1390-1396.

Baker, H.S., & M.N. Baker. 1987. "Heinz Kohut's Self Psychology: An Overview." *American Journal of Psychiatry* 144 (1): 1-9.

Barry, H. Jr., H. Barry, III, & E. Lindemann. 1965. Dependency in Adult Patients Following Early Maternal Bereavement. *Journal of Nervous and Mental Disease* 140: 196-206.

Bennis, W.G., & H.A. Shepard. 1956. A Theory of Group Development. *Human Relations* 9: 415-457.

Benyamini, K. 1987. Professional Behavior During Conditions of Extreme Community Turmoil: The Case of the Removal of Settlements from Sinai. *Journal of Applied Behavioral Science* 23 (1): 131-137.

Berenbeim, R.F. 1985. "Company Programs to Ease the Impact of Shutdowns." *The Conference Board* (A Research Report): 1-57.

Berg, D.N. 1985. Anxiety in Research Relationships. In D.N. Berg and K.K. Smith (Eds), *Exploring Clinical Methods for Social Research*, pp. 213-228. Beverly Hills: Sage Publications.

Berg, D.N. & K.K. Smith, (Eds). 1985. *Exploring Clinical Methods for Social Research*. Beverly Hills: Sage Publications.

Bion, W.R. 1961. *Experiences in Groups*. London: Tavistock Publications.

Bloom-Feshbach, J., & S. Bloom-Feshbach. 1987. Afterword: Converging Themes in the Psychology of Separation and Loss. In J. Bloom-Feshbach & S. Bloom-Feshbach (Eds.), *The Psychology of Separation and Loss*, San Francisco: Jossey-Bass.

Boulian, P.V. 1974. *Symbolization in Organizational Life*. Doctoral Dissertation, Yale University: New Haven, Connecticut.

Bowen, M. 1978. On the Differentiation of Self. In Bowen, M. *Family Therapy in Clinical Practice*, Chapter 21. New York: Jason Aronson.

Bowlby, J. 1969. *Attachment and Loss*, Volume I: *Attachment*. New York: Basic Books.

Bowlby, J. 1973a. *Attachment and Loss*, Volume II: *Separation*. New York: Basic Books.

Bowlby, J. 1973b. Separation Anxiety: Review of the Literature. In J. Bowlby, *Attachment and Loss*, Volume II: *Separation*, Appendix 1, pp. 375-398. New York: Basic Books.

Bowlby, J. 1975. Attachment Theory, Separation Anxiety, and Mourning. In D.A. Hamburg and H.K.H. Brodie (Eds.), *American Handbook of Psychiatry Volume VI: New Psychiatric Frontiers*, pp. 292-309. New York: Basic Books.

Bowlby, J. 1980. *Attachment and Loss*, Volume III: *Loss*. New York: Basic Books.

Bowlby, J. 1988a. Developmental Psychiatry Comes of Age. *American Journal of Psychiatry* 145 (1): 1-10.

Bowlby, J. 1988b. *A Secure Base*. New York: Basic Books.

Bradburn, N.M., L.J. Rips,& S.K. Shevell. 1987. Answering Autobiographical Questions: The Impact of Memory and Inference on Surveys. *Science* 236 (Apr. 10): 157-161.

Brockner, J., S. Grover, T. Reed, R. DeWitt, & M. O'Malley. 1987. Survivors' Reactions to Layoffs: We Get by with a Little Help for Our Friends. *Administrative Science Quarterly* 32: 526-541.

Buono, A.F., J.L. Bowditch, & J.L. Lewis, III. 1985. When Cultures Collide: The Anatomy of a Merger. *Human Relations* 38 (5): 477-500.

Burlingham, D., & A. Freud. 1944. *Infants Without Families*. London: Allen and Unwin.

Burlingham, D., & A. Freud. 1942. *Young Children in Wartime*. London: Allen and Unwin.

Callahan, J.P. 1986. Chemistry: How Mismatched Managements Can Kill a Deal. *Mergers and Acquisitions*, Mar./Apr.: 47-53.

Dasberg, H., & G. Sheffler. 1987. The Disbandment of a Community: A Psychiatric Action Research Project. *Journal of Applied Behavioral Science* 23 (1): 89-101.

Davenport, R.K. Jr., E. W. Menzel, Jr., & C.M. Rogers. 1966. Effects of Severe Isolation on "Normal" Juvenile Chimpanzees. *Archives of General Psychiatry* 14 (Feb.): 134-138.

DeCasper, A.J., and W.P. Fifier. 1980. Of Human Bonding: Infants Prefer Their Mothers' Voices. *Science* 208 (Jun.): 1174-1176.

DeMeuse, K.P. 1986. Merger Mania: Anatomy of a Corporate Takeover {A Researcher's Perspective}. Presented at the American Psychological Association annual meeting, Washington, D.C., Aug. 25.

Deutsch, M., & R.M. Krauss. 1962. Studies of Interpersonal Bargaining. *Journal of Conflict Resolution* 6: 52-67.

Dobryzinski, J.H. 1988. A New Strain of Merger Mania. *Business Week*, Mar. 21: 122-126.

Doris, J., A. McIntyre, & M. Tarnoff. 1980. Separation Anxiety in Preschool Children: Chapter 17. In I.L. Kutash, & L.B. Schlesinger (Eds.) *Handbook on Stress and Anxiety: Contemporary Knowledge, Theory, and Treatment*, pp. 298-316. San Francisco: Jossey-Bass.

Dumas, Alexander (the Elder). 1844. *The Three Musketeers*.

Eliot, T.S. 1934. *The Waste Land and Other Poems*. New York: Harcourt, Brace and World.

Festinger, L. 1957. *A Theory of Cognitive Dissonance*. New York: Row, Peterson.

Forbes. 1988. Review of Merger Transactions. Mergers and Acquisitions Special Advertising Section, May.

Freud, A. 1937. *The Ego and Its Mechanisms of Defense*. London: Hogarth Press.

Freud, A. 1945. Indications for Child Analysis. In *The Psychoanalytic Study of the Child*, Volume 1, pp. 127-149. New York: International Universities Press.

Freud, S. 1909. Analysis of a Phobia in a Five-Year-Old Boy. In J. Strachey (Ed.) *Standard Edition*, Volume 10, pp. 3-149. London: Hogarth Press, 1955.

Freud, S. 1925. *The Problem of Anxiety*. Translated by H.A. Bunker. New York: W.W. Norton, 1936.

Freud, S. 1936. Inhibitions, Symptoms, and Anxiety. In J. Strachey (Ed.) *Standard Edition*, Volume 20. London: Hogarth Press, 1955.

Freud, S. 1917. *Mourning and Melancholia*. London: Hogarth Press, 1974.

Freund, R.J., R.C. Littell, & P.C. Spector. 1986. *SAS System for Linear Models*. Cary, N.C.: SAS Institute Inc.

Gersick, C.J.G. 1985. *Time and Transition in Work Teams: Towards a New Model of Group Development*. Unpublished Manuscript, UCLA Graduate School of Management.

Goleman, D. 1987. Terror's Children: Mending Mental Wounds. *New York Times*, Feb. 24, pp. C-1, C-12.

Greenhouse, S.W., & S. Geisser. 1959. On Methods in the Analysis of Profile Data. *Psychometrika* 32 (3): 95-112.

Haley, J. 1980. *Leaving Home: The Therapy of Disturbed Young People*. New York: McGraw-Hill.

Hamburg, D.A. 1969. A Perspective on Coping. Paper presented at the Conference on Coping and Adaptation, Stanford University, Mar.

Harlow, H.F. 1958. The Nature of Love. *American Psychologist* 13: 673-685.

Harlow, H.F. 1974. *Learning to Love*. New York: Jason Aronson.

Harlow, H.F., & M. Harlow. 1965. The Affectional Systems. In A. Schrier, H.F. Harlow, & F. Stollnitz (Eds.) *Behavior of Nonhuman Primates*, Volume II. New York: Academic Press.

Harlow, H.F., & R.R. Zimmerman. 1959. Affectional Responses in the Infant Monkey. *Science* 130: 421-432.

Harshbarger, D. 1987. Takeover: A Tale of Loss Change and Growth. *Academy of Management Executive* 1 (4): 339-343.

Hayes, R.H. 1979. The Human Side of Acquisitions. *Academy of Management Review* Nov.: 41-46.

Henn, F.A.M., L.W. Krinsky, & L. J. Warshaw. 1989. *Change at the Top: The Effects of Corporate Mergers, Takeovers, and Management Changes*. New York: Maple Hill Press.

Herbert, J.I. 1989. *Black Male Entrepreneurs and Adult Development*. New York: Prager Publishers.

Herbert, J.I., & J.H. Astrachan. 1988. An Intergroup Simulation: The Collared Exercise. Unpublished manuscript.

Hofer, M.A. 1975. The Principles of Autonomic Function in the Life of Man and Animals. In M.F. Reiser (Ed.), *American Handbook of Psychiatry Volume IV: Organic Disorders and Psychosomatic Medicine*, pp. 528-552, New York: Basic Books.

Holmes, R.E. 1988. How to Retain Work Forces When Firms are Acquired. *Mergers and Acquisitions*, Mar./Apr.: 61-63.

House, J.S., K.R. Landis, & D. Umberson. 1988. Social Relationships and Health. *Science* 241 (Jul. 29): 540-545.

Huynh, H., & L.S. Feldt. 1970. Conditions Under Which Mean Square Ratios in Repeated Measures Designs Have Exact F-Distributions. *Journal of the American Statistical Association* 65: 1582-1589.

Jacobs, S.C., T.R. Kosten, S.V. Kasl, A.M. Ostfeld, L. Berkman, & P. Charpentier. 1987-88. Attachment Theory and Multiple Dimensions of Grief. *Omega* 18 (1): 41-52.

James, W. 1902. *The Varieties of Religious Experience*. New York: Random House.

Janis, I.L. 1963. Group Identification Under Conditions of External Danger. *British Journal of Medical Psychology* 36: 227-238.

Janis, I.L. 1958. *Psychological Stress*. New York: Wiley.

Janis, I.L. 1972. *Victims of Groupthink: A Psychological Study of Foreign Policy Decisions and Fiascoes*. Boston: Houghton Mifflin Co.

Jaques, E. 1974. Social Systems as a Defense Against Persecutory and Depressive Anxiety. In G.S. Gibbard, J.J. Hartman, & R.D. Mann (Eds.), *Analysis of Group's Contributions to Theory Research and Practice*. London: Jossey-Bass.

Joyce, E. 1988. *Prime Times, Bad Times*. New York: Doubleday.

Keller, R.T. & W.E. Holland. 1981. Job Change: A Naturally Occurring Field Experiment. *Human Relations* 34 (12): 1053-1067.

Klein, M. 1948. *Contributions to Psychoanalysis*. London: Hogarth.

Kotter, J.P. 1973. The Psychological Contract: Managing the Joining-Up Process. *California Management Review* 15 (3): 91-99.

Krantz, J. 1985. Groups Process Under Conditions of Organizational Decline. *Journal of Applied Behavioral Science* 21 (1): 1-17.

Krupnick, J.L., & F. Solomon. 1987. Death of a Parent or Sibling During Childhood. In J. Bloom-Feshbach and S. Bloom-Feshback (Eds.), *The Psychology of Separation and Loss*, pp. 345-371. San Francisco: Jossey Bass.

Kubler-Ross, E. 1969. *On Death and Dying*. London: Macmillan.

Kuypers, B.C., D. Davies, & A. Hazewinkel. 1986. Developmental Patterns in Self-Analytic Groups. *Human Relations* 39 (9): 793-815.

Lansberg, I. 1989. Social Categorization, Entitlement, and Justice in Organizations: Contextual Determinants and Cognitive Underpinnings. *Human Relations* 41 (12): 871-899.

Lawick-Goodall, J. van. 1968. The Behaviour of Free Ranging Chimpanzees in the Gombe Stream Reserve. *Animal Behaviour Monographs* 1: 161-311.

Leff, M.J., J.F. Roatch, & W.E. Bunney, Jr. 1970. Environmental Factors Preceding the Onset of Severe Depressions. *Psychiatry* 33 (3): 293-311.

Lesse, S. 1970. *Anxiety—Its Components, Development and Treatment.* New York: Grune and Stratton.

Lesse, S. 1982. The Relationship of Anxiety to Depression. *American Journal of Psychotherapy* 36 (3): 332-349.

Levinson, D.J. 1986. A Conception of Adult Development. *American Psychologist* 41 (1): 3-13.

Levinson, D.J., with C.N. Darrow, E.B. Klein, M.H. Levinson, & B. McKee. 1978. *The Seasons of A Man's Life.* New York: Knopf.

Levinson, H. 1970. A Psychologist Diagnoses Merger Failures. *Harvard Business Review,* Mar./Apr.: 139-147.

Levinson, H. 1972. Easing the Pain of Personal Loss. *Harvard Business Review,* Sept./Oct.: 80-88.

Lewis, A.J. 1970. Problems Presented by the Ambiguous Word 'Anxiety' as Used in Psychopathology. *International Journal of Psychiatry* 9: 62-79.

Lewis, J.K., W.T. McKinney, Jr., L.D. Young, & G.W. Kraemer. 1976. Mother-Infant Separation in Rhesus Monkeys as Model of Human Depression. *Archives of General Psychiatry* 33 (Jun.): 699-705.

Lichter, R.L. 1988. Ph.D. Candidates Need Faculties That Care. *New York Times,* Jan. 4, p. A-18.

MacLean, P.D. 1985. Brain Evolution Relating to Family, Play, and the Separation Call. *Archives of General Psychiatry* 42 (Apr.): 405-417.

Madrick, J. 1988. 'Wall Street': The Banality of Greed. *The New York Times,* Jan. 17, Business Section, p. 2.

Mahler, M., F. Pine, & A. Bergman. 1975. *The Psychological Birth of the Human Infant.* New York: Basic Books.

Marks, M.L. 1982. Merging Human Resources: A Review of Current Research. *Mergers and Acquisitions,* Summer: 38-44.

Marks, M.L., & P.H. Mirvis. 1985. Merger Syndrome: Stress and Uncertainty. *Mergers and Acquisitions,* Summer: 50-55.

Marris, P. 1974. *Loss and Change.* New York: Pantheon Books.

May, R. 1977. *The Meaning of Anxiety (revised edition).* New York: Washington Square Press.

McCabe, P. 1987. *Bad News at Black Rock.* New York: Arbor House.

McKinney, W.T. Jr. 1974. Primate Social Isolation: Psychiatric Implication. *Archives of General Psychiatry* 31 (Sept.): 422-426.

McMillan, S.D. 1981. An Application of Turquet's Basic-Assumption Oneness in the Analysis of a Group in Search of Utopia. *Human Relations* 34 (6): 475-490.

Meares, R. 1986. On the Ownership of Thought: An Approach to the Origins of Separation Anxiety. *Psychiatry* 49 (Feb.): 80-91.

Merrell, D.W. 1986. Merger Mania: A Consultant's Perspective. Presented at the American Psychological Association Annual Meeting, Aug. 25.

Miller, E.J. 1959. Technology, Territory, and Time. *Human Relations* 12: 243-272.

Mirvis, P.H., & M.L. Marks. 1986. Merger Syndrome: Management by Crisis, Part II. *Mergers and Acquisitions*, Jan./Feb.: 70-76.

Moberly, E.R. 1986. Attachment and Separation: The Implications for Gender Identity and the Structuralization of the Self: A Theoretical Model for Transexualism and Homosexuality. *Psychiatry Journal of the University of Ottowa* 11 (4): 205-209.

Moreland, R.L. 1985. Social Categorization and the Assimilation of "New" Group Members. *Journal of Personality and Social Psychology* 48 (5): 1173-1190.

Morrison, D.F. 1976. *Multivariate Statistical Methods, Second Edition.* New York: McGraw-Hill.

Moses, R., J.M. Rosenfeld, & R. Moses-Hrushovski. 1987. Facing the Threat of Removal: Lessons from the Forced Evacuation of Ofira. *Journal of Applied Behavioral Science* 23 (1): 53-71.

Mowday, R.T. 1981. Viewing Turnover From the Perspective of Those Who Remain: The Relationship of Job Attitudes to Attributions of the Causes of Turnover. *Journal of Applied Psychology* 66 (2): 120-123.

Myers, D.G., & H. Lamm. 1975. The Polarizing Effect of Group Discussion. *American Scientist* 13 (May/Jun.): 297-303.

Nash, N.C. 1988. Company Buyouts Assailed in Study. *New York Times*, Jan. 31, p. A31.

Nussbaum, B., K. Failla, C.S. Eklund, A. Beam, J.R. Norman, & K. Deveny. 1986. The End of Corporate Loyalty? *Business Week*, Aug. 4, pp. 40-49.

Parkes, C.M. 1975. Psycho-social Transitions: Comparison between Reactions to Loss of a Limb and Loss of a Spouse. *British Journal of Psychiatry* 127: 204-210.

Parkes, C.M. 1969. Separation Anxiety: An Aspect of the Search for a Lost Object. In M.H. Lader (Ed.), *Studies of Anxiety, British Journal of Psychiatry Special Publication* 3, pp. 87-92.

Parkes, C.M. 1972. *Bereavement: Studies of Grief in Adult Life.* New York: International Universities Press.

Peterson, R.G. 1977. Use and Misuse of Multiple Comparison Procedures. *Agronomy Journal* 69: 205-208.

Pollock, M.A. 1986. The Disposable Employee is Becoming a Fact of Corporate Life. *Business Week*, Dec. 15, pp. 52-56.

Rank, O. 1924, English translation 1929. *The Trauma of Birth.* London: Kegan Paul.

Rey, D.R., Jr. 1972. Change of Command in Combat: A Locus of Stress. *American Journal of Psychiatry* 126 (6): 698-702.

Rheingold, H.L., & C.O. Eckerman. 1970. The Infant Separates Himself from His Mother. *Science* 168 (Apr.): 78-83.

Rice, A.K. 1969. Individual, Group, and Intergroup Processes. *Human Relations* 22 (6): 565-584.

Romzek, B.S. 1985. The Effects of Public Service Recognition, Job Security, and Staff Reductions on Organizational Involvement. *Public Administration Review*, Mar./Apr.: 282-291.

Rosenthal, S. 1985. Mourning and Depression in Organizations. In V. Volkan (Ed.), pp. 201-219. *Depressive States and Their Treatment*, New York: Jason Aronson.

Roy, A. 1985. Early Parental Loss and Adult Depression. *Archives of General Psychiatry* 42 (Oct.): 987-991.

Roy-Byrne, P.P., M. Geraci, & T.W. Uhde. 1986. Life Events and the Onset of Panic Disorder. *American Journal of Psychiatry* 143 (11): 1424-1427.

Safire, W. 1986. The Crisis of Institutional Loyalty. *New York Times*, Aug. 18, p. A17.

Schacter, S. 1959. *The Psychology of Affiliation*. Stanford: Stanford University Press.

Schacter, S., & J.E. Singer. 1962. Cognitive and Psychological Determinants of Emotional State. *Psychological Review* 69: 379-399.

Schlenker, J.A., & B.A. Gutek. 1987. Effects of Role Loss on Work-Related Attitudes. *Journal of Applied Psychology* 72 (2): 287-293.

Schmale, A.H. 1958. Relationship of Separation and Depression to Disease: A Report on a Hospitalized Medical Population. *Psychosomatic Medicine* 20: 259-277.

Seligman, M.E.P. 1975. *Helplessness*. San Francisco: W.H. Freeman and Company.

Sherif, M. 1958. Superordinate Goals in the Reduction of Intergroup Conflict. *American Journal of Sociology* 63: 349-358.

Siehl, C., G. Ledford, R. Silverman, & P. Fay. 1988. Preventing Culture Clashes from Botching a Merger. *Mergers and Acquisitions*, Mar./Apr.: 51-57.

Sinetar, M. 1981. Mergers, Morale, and Productivity. *Personnel Journal*, Nov.: 863-867.

Skinner, B.F. (with W.K. Estes). 1941. Some Quantitative Properties of Anxiety. *Journal of Experimental Psychology* 29: 390-400.

Sklar, A.D., & R.F. Harris. 1985. Effects of Parent Loss: Interaction With Family Size and Sibling Order. *American Journal of Psychiatry* 124 (6): 708-714.

Smith, E.T., J. Brott, A. Cuneo, & J.E. Davis. 1988. Stress: The Test Americans are Failing. *Business Week*, Apr. 18, pp. 74-76.

Solomon, C. 1989. Lingering Shock: Takeover Raids Leave Phillips Employees Fearing New Assaults. *Wall Street Journal*, Feb. 1, pp. 1, 8.

Steinglass, P., A.K. De-Nour, & S. Shye. 1985. Factors Influencing Psychosocial Adjustment to Forced Geographical Relocation: The Israeli Withdrawl from the Sinai. *American Journal of Orthopsychiatry* 55 (4): 513-529.

Steinglass, P., E. Weisstub, & A.K. De-Nour. 1986. Perceived Personal Networks as Mediators of Stress Reactions. Paper presented to The American Psychiatric Association Annual Meeting, May 10-16.

Stierlin, H. 1974. *Separating Parents and Adolescents*, New York: Quadrangle.

Suomi, S.J., H.F. Harlow, & W.T. Mckinney, Jr. 1972. Monkey Psychiatrists. *American Journal of Psychiatry* 128 (8): 41-46.

Sutton, R.I. 1987. The Process of Organizational Death: Disbanding and Reconnecting. *Administrative Science Quarterly* 32: 542-569.

Tajfel, H. 1970. Experiments in Intergroup Discrimination. *Scientific American* 223: 96-102.

Tennant, C., A. Smith, P. Bebbington, & J. Hurry. 1981. Parental Loss in Childhood. *Archives of General Psychiatry* 38 March: 309-314.

Thomas, D.A. 1986. *An Intra-Organizational Analysis of Differences in Black and White Patterns of Sponsorship and the Dynamics of Cross-Racial Mentoring.* Doctoral Dissertation, Yale University: New Haven, Connecticut.

Thomas, E.J., & C.F. Fink. 1963. Effects of Group Size. *Psychological Bulletin* 60 (4): 371-384.

Tomasko, R.M. 1988. The Right Way to Shrink a Company. *The New York Times*, Jan. 10, Business Section, p. 2.

Tuckman, B.W. 1965. Developmental Sequence in Small Groups. *Psychological Bulletin* 63: 384-399.

Turner, C.H., R.K. Davenport, Jr., & C.M. Rogers. 1969. The Effect of Early Deprivation on the Social Behavior of Adolescent Chimpanzees. *American Journal of Psychiatry* 125 (11): 85-90.

Turquet, P. 1975. Threats to Identity in the Large Group. In L. Kreeger (Ed.) *The Large Group: Dynamics and Therapy*, pp. 87-144. London: Constable.

Uhde, T.W., J. Boulenger, L.J. Slever, R.L. DuPont, & R.M. Post. 1982. Animal Models of Anxiety: Implications for Research in Humans. *Psychopharmacology Bulletin* 18 (4): 47-52.

Van Steenberg, V. 1988. *Organizational Exits.* Doctoral Dissertation, Yale University: New Haven, Connecticut.

Weiss, R.S. 1975. *Marital Separation: Managing After a Marriage Ends.* New York: Basic Books.

Wells, A.S. 1988. The Never-Ending Dissertation. *New York Times* (Education Supplement), p. EDUC-59-63.

Winer, B.J. 1962. *Statistical Principles in Experimental Design.* New York: McGraw-Hill.

Winnicott, D.W. 1953. Transitional Objects and Transitional Phenomena: A Study of the First Not-Me Possessions. *International Journal of Psychoanalysis*, pp. 34.

Yang, J.E. 1988. Bill on Plant Closings and Layoffs Clears Senate in New Effort and Trade Measure. *Wall Street Journal*, Jul. 7, p. 50.

Yarrow, L. 1967. The Development of Focused Relationships During Infancy. In J. Hellmuth (Ed.) *The Exceptional Infant*, Volume 1. New York: Brunner/Mazel.

Young, L.D., S.S. Suomi, H.F. Harlow, & W.T. McKinney, Jr. 1973. Early Stress and Later Response to Separation in Rhesus Monkeys. *American Journal of Psychiatry* 130 (4): 400-405.

Ziller, R.C. 1965. Toward a Theory of Open and Closed Groups. *Psychological Bulletin* 34 (3): 164-182.

Index

About the Author

JOSEPH H. ASTRACHAN, Ph.D., serves as associate director of the Center for Management at The Institute of Living and co-director of the Southern New England Family Business Forum, in Hartford, Connecticut. He has consulted to businesses and nonprofit organizations on inter-group conflict, challenges associated with gender relations, race relations, mergers and acquisitions, and the management of family-owned businesses. His publications and research interests include the management of family-owned firms and professional organizations, gender relations, race relations, and human reactions to organizational change. Dr. Astrachan is active in the Family Firm Institute and is the interview editor for the *Family Business Review*. He is a member of the faculty of the Owner Managed Business Institute, Santa Barbara, California. Dr. Astrachan earned degrees in social psychology and organizational behavior from Yale University and the Yale School of Organization and Management.